Academic Freedom

The Editor

Anna S. Ochoa is Professor of Education at Indiana University, Bloomington.

The Advisory Panel

Nancy R. Brown, Chairperson, FTP-NEA Committee on Censorship, Micanopy, Florida

Earl E. Harrington, English/Social Studies Teacher, Central Middle School, Plymouth-Canton Community Schools, Plymouth, Michigan

Peter L. Hildebrand, Sixth Grade Teacher, Gates School, Acton, Massachusetts

Sue Karahalios, Educator, Oak Harbor Middle School, Washington

Sally Miller, Media Specialist, Doherty High School, Colorado Springs, Colorado

Lee J. Rednock, Chair, Pennsylvania New Right Task Force, and Earth and Space Science Teacher, Western Pennsylvania

Academic Freedom
to teach and to learn:
Every Teacher's Issue

Anna S. Ochoa, Editor

Appendix by Janet L. Jones

nea PROFESSIONAL LIBRARY
National Education Association
Washington, D.C.

Printing History
    First Printing: June 1990

Note

The opinions expressed in this publication should not be construed as representing the policy or position of the National Education Association. Materials published by the NEA Professional Library are intended to be discussion documents for teachers who are concerned with specialized interests of the profession.

Library of Congress Cataloging-in-Publication Data

Academic freedom to teach and to learn : every teacher's issue / Anna
    S. Ochoa, editor.
        p.   cm. — (Aspects of learning)
    Includes bibliographical references.
    ISBN 0-8106-3006-0
        1. Academic freedom—United States.   2. Teaching, Freedom of—
United States.   3. Freedom of information—United States.
4. Censorship—United States.   I. Ochoa, Anna.   II. Series.
LC72.2.A33   1990
371.1'04—dc20   90-35524
                                                                      CIP

CONTENTS

NEA Policy on Academic and Professional Freedom

NEA Resolution

E-6. Academic and Professional Freedom

The National Education Association believes that academic freedom is essential to the teaching profession. Academic freedom includes the rights of teachers and learners to explore and discuss divergent points of view. Controversial issues should be a part of the instructional program when, in the judgment of the professional staff, the issues are appropriate to the curriculum and to the maturity level of the student.

The Association also believes that professional freedom is essential to the teaching profession. Professional freedom includes the teachers' right to evaluate, criticize, and/or advocate their personal point of view concerning the policies and programs of the schools. Teachers also have the right to assist colleagues when their academic or professional freedoms are violated.

The Association further believes that legislation and regulations that mandate or permit the teaching of religious doctrines and/or groups that promote antipublic education agendas violate both student and teacher rights. The Association urges its affiliates to seek repeal of these mandates where they exist. (69, 86)

INTRODUCTION

by Anna S. Ochoa, Professor of Education, Indiana University

I first encountered the significance of academic freedom as an undergraduate preparing to be a social studies teacher. A required methods course provided many opportunities for probing the vagaries of teaching and learning. One class meeting remains indelibly imprinted in my memory. A poignant film that emphasized intellectual freedom and censorship served as the centerpiece for that session. Until then neither I, nor my classmates, had given any serious thought to the challenges of teaching that are associated with intellectual expression. Using dramatic footage, the film depicted teachers in Nazi Germany being muzzled by the oppressive practices of the Third Reich. These teachers were under orders not to teach designated topics. In addition, books were burned to "protect" German youth from "undesirable" ideas. For those of us who were neophyte teachers, these dramatic scenes created a new reality of what being a teacher really means. They permitted all of us to capture a harsh glimpse of the consequences of rampant censorship.

Especially moving was the portrayal of the unusually courageous resistance demonstrated by some of these German teachers. Despite the clear and imminent threat of punishment—many of them were ultimately arrested and imprisoned—they showed the determination and courage necessary to conduct their classrooms with academic honesty. All of us watching the film were convinced, as Americans often are, that such severe conditions were not likely to happen here. At the same time, we left that room more aware that there was always the possibility that Americans were not exempt from censorship. And privately we wondered whether we were capable of mustering the same strength and courage displayed by these dedicated teachers.

The essential message of the film for me was that teaching was indeed a very special occupation and that teachers serve as guardians of democracy. They have the awesome responsibility of shaping the minds of the next generation. Our democrtatic system, to a considerable degree, depends on the professional courage and determination of our teachers.

When teachers select content and experiences for their students, they can, on the one hand, act in behalf of democratic principles and the free expression of ideas or, on the other hand, they can act in ways that inhibit them. In essence, teaching in a democratic society can be symbolized as a crucible for seeking truth, for sharing with the next generation the best of what is known, for presenting controversial points of view, and for developing young citizens who are thoughtful, independent, and critical. With these abilities, students will be sufficiently strong so that they cannot be manipulated, indoctrinated, or coerced.

For me, as well as my peers, the film brought our roles as teachers into sharp focus. As teachers we would not merely be dispensers of knowledge and teaching was not just an occupation. Rather, teachers can and must serve to protect and probe all ideas. Student-citizens must be exposed to a wide range of views and positions, ones we love as well as some we hate, and each of us, in our own classrooms, must see ourselves as seekers of "truth" and open inquiry. Teaching as a profession calls for courage and integrity, not unlike the courage displayed by resisting teachers in Nazi Germany. And time has taught us that censorship not only can, but has, happened here.

We have learned that even in this society, books have been burned and teachers have been fired. Though these practices have not been initiated or sanctioned by the national government as they were in Nazi Germany, they have had serious negative effects on students, teachers and, as important, on the freedom to learn and the freedom to teach. Controversial topics have been avoided, books have been removed from library shelves, and teachers have been frightened. Although no one has been imprisoned, people have been victimized.

All of us who teach need to remember (and, I might add, should never forget) the unsung heros of the teaching profession. Over time, substantial numbers of teachers have acted vigorously and courageously. In the face of angry parents, threatening school boards, and even unsympathetic courts, they have defended their positions and have been subjected to harassment and criticisms. All of this notwithstanding, they have stood their ground. They have sometimes won and sometimes lost. When they have won, we, all of us in the teaching profession, as well as our students, have won. And when they have lost, democratic principles and cherished freedoms have been lost for students and teachers as well.

These instances of courage represent the hallmark of the profession. Indeed, they symbolize the profession at its best—resolute, determined, and dedicated to freedom of ideas. No one has built monuments to these teachers (though they probably should), but clearly, if there were ever to be a Teaching Hall of Fame, these individuals would stand tallest of all.

To balance the picture, we must necessarily turn to the other side of the matter. Without question, instances of teacher self-censorship abound. No one knows how often teachers privately say to themselves: "I can't use that book—it's just too controversial." "Teach about evolution in THIS community, you've got to be kidding!" "Talk about the terrible environmental impact of the local chemical plant—of course not! I'd get fired!'' The persistent wave of censorship affecting classroom content, classroom methods, textbooks, library books, and student newspapers causes teachers to be increasingly cautious, to avoid the controversial, and to play it safe.

Freedom to teach and freedom to learn remain in danger. Tragically, however, they are not only susceptible to erosion because of censorship efforts from the right wing, and sometimes, from the left, but also they are eroding because many educators are not prepared to deal with partisan attacks. Lack of procedures and guidelines established by the school boards is but one example. Consequently, there are many instances where a teacher, a principal, a superintendent, or a school board virtually shrivel and give in at the first sign of community concern. Educators much too often want to keep the peace and maintain harmony, and too often they easily compromise the quality of academic freedom by default. They simply don't put up a fight.

At the same time, there are cases to the contrary. Teresa Burnau, an English teacher in Warsaw, Indiana, is one example described by Edward Jenkinson in his chapter, ''Lessons Learned from Three Schoolbook Protests.'' H. Keith Sterzing is another. Sterzing, a Texas social studies teacher, challenged his dismissal from his school district (for teaching controversial issues) and won. Both Burnau and Sterzing ultimately left the teaching profession—an understandable, but tragic outcome. While we can't all fight the challenge as Burnau and Sterzing did, we can assume the very serious responsibility of preparing ourselves for criticisms and attacks on our teaching methods and materials.

This publication is devoted to that mission. It is the fervent hope of this editor and the authors that the contents of this book will help educators at all levels to act in more informed and courageous ways regarding the issues and forces impinging on intellectual freedom.

To that end, this book provides chapters that deal with the scope of censorship issues, the significance of academic freedom, a review of recent judicial rulings, an examination of school-community tensions, and a final chapter that presents three case studies of censorship cases.

1. CHILD ABUSE IN THE HATE FACTORY

by Edward B. Jenkinson, Professor of English Education,
Indiana University

The mythical public school may be in your neighborhood. Be it elementary or secondary, the "government seminary" as it is called by several prominent critics of public education is controlled by "change agents." They are individuals whose goal is "to change the beliefs, values, attitudes or behavior of people without their knowledge or consent."[1]

Barbara M. Morris, an outspoken critic of "government education" and its "change agents," declared:

> The purpose of most of the activity that takes place in public, and often, in private and church schools, is not to change the child by developing his intellect, teaching him skills and a traditional body of knowledge. Rather, the purpose is to eliminate existing traditional beliefs, values, attitudes and behaviors and to replace them with beliefs and behaviors that will render the child susceptible to manipulation, coercion, control and corruption for the rest of his life.[2]

Strong words? Of course. Diatribes are rarely couched in timid language. Believable? Not to teachers who know the schools intimately. But Morris and others like her do not write for teachers. They write for people who sometimes may, but more likely will not, verify charges.

A prime example of the propagandists who blast public schools with their rhetoric is the Reverend Tim LaHaye. One of the founders of the now defunct Moral Majority, he is the author of the "battle" series of books about the evils of secular humanism. Each of three of his "battle" books has sold more than one hundred thousand copies, and each stirs the reader with an endless string of messages like these:

> Secular educators no longer make learning their primary objective. Instead our public schools have become conduits to the minds of our youth, training them to be anti-God, anti-moral, anti-family, anti-free enterprise and anti-American.[3]
>
> Public education today is a self-serving institution controlled by elitists of an atheistic, humanistic viewpoint; they are more interested in indoctrinating their charges against the recognition of God, absolute moral values, and a belief in the American dream than they are in teaching them to read, write, and do arithmetic. I call these people humanist educrats.[4]

Sound familiar? Echoes of Barbara Morris can be heard throughout New Right literature about the public schools. That does not mean that the charges originated with her. Rather, it means that many critics hurl essentially the same barbs in slightly different language. For the goal is the same: to totally discredit public education and its teachers.

Erica Carle started her condemnation with the title *The Hate Factory*. In it she charged:

> Young people are being corrupted, discouraged, deflated, frustrated, over-burdened, and deceived. If you are a parent you need to find out who is trying to alienate your children's affection and persuade them to abandon the principles you have taught them. You need to find out who is teaching the young to hate family loyalty, Christian morality and Christian individuals, hate honest scientific investigation, hate independence, self-responsiblity and achievement. You need to know so that you can take protective measures.

Let us go to the place where the persuaders do much of their work. Let us go with the children to the hate factory to their sociology classroom.[3]

The mythical school now has another wing—sociology. Fortunately, not very many parents jumped on the Carle bandwagon and tried to drive sociology out of town. One of the reasons for their lack of effort may have been that they could not find a course in sociology in the local school. But Carle noted that it may not be called sociology; its message of hate, she wrote, is also being spread through social studies and future studies.

Another evil, according to a New Right leader, is psychology. In a televised sermon in May 1989, the Reverend D. James Kennedy, pastor of the Coral Gables (Florida) Presbyterian Church, denounced psychology as a religion. An opponent of secular humanism, Dr. Kennedy has added yet another religion that his followers should search for in the public schools. New Right critics have already charged, especially during the mid- to late eighties, that the schools are preaching these religions: secular humanism, New Age, and globalism.

Phyllis Schlafly, perhaps the best known of all of the New Right critics of public education, has mobilized thousands in her attempts to change the schools. Members of her Eagle Forum have fought secular humanism, the New Age, sex education, global education, and other perceived evils in school board meetings throughout the nation. The title of her best-selling book, *Child Abuse in the Classroom*, is in itself an indictment of public schools. She compiled and edited the transcripts of the 1984 hearings that the Department of Education conducted on the Hatch Amendment. Four paragraphs from her introduction encapsulate more than a dozen charges of the critics and reflect the contempt that she and her followers have for public education:

11

These Hearings explain why the American people are so dissatisfied with schools today. These Hearings explain *why* we have 23 million adult illiterates who graduated from public schools, and *why* young people are experiencing high rates of teenage suicide, loneliness, premarital sex, and pregnancies.

These Hearings explain *how* schools have alienated children from their parents, from traditional morality such as the Ten Commandments, and from our American heritage. These hearings explain *why* children are so emotionally and morally confused and *why*, in the apt colloquialism, they need to "search for their identity."

These Hearings explain *what* children have been doing in their classrooms instead of learning to read, write, spell, add, subtract, and the essentials of history, geography, and civics. These Hearings explain how children learn in school to be "sexually active," take illegal drugs, repudiate their parents, and rationalize immoral and anti-social conduct when it "feels" good in a particular "situation."

These Hearings speak with the thunderous voice of hundreds of parents who are angry at how their children have been emotionally, morally, and intellectually abused by psychological and behavioral experiments during classroom hours when the parents *thought* their children were being taught basic knowledge skills. Parents are indignant at the way that educator "change agents," spending federal tax dollars, have used children as guinea pigs for fads and experiments that have been substituted for real learning.[6]

Phyllis Schlafly, Barbara M. Morris, Erica Carle, D. James Kennedy, and Tim LaHaye—along with televangelists Pat Robertson, Jerry Falwell, and Jimmy Swaggart—have helped to build that mythical school in your neighborhood. They have contributed to the dissatisfaction of hundreds of parents who distrust public education. And they are not alone. Other authors have added books to the "hate the schools" bookshelf. Here are only 10 titles that I have in my study:

William M. Bowen, Jr., *Globalism: America's Demise.* Shreveport, La.: Huntington House, 1984.

Homer Dunan, *The Religion of Secular Humanism and the Public Schools.* Lubbock, Tex.: MC International Publications, second printing, 1986.

Mel Gabler, and Norma Gabler with James C. Hefley, *What Are They Teaching Our Children?* Wheaton, Ill.: Victor Books, 1985.

James C. Hefley, *Are Textbooks Harming Your Children?* Milford, Mich.: Mott Media, 1979.

Robert Allen Hill, and Olaf John, *Your Children: The Victims of Public Education.* Van Nuys, Calif.: Bible Voice, 1978.

Texe Marrs, *Dark Secrets of the New Age: Satan's Plan for a One World Religion.* Westchester, Ill.: Crossway Books, 1987.

Connaught Coyne Marshner, *Blackboard Tyranny*. New Rochelle, N.Y.: Arlington House, 1978.

Opal Moore, *Why Can't Johnny Learn?* Milford, Mich.: Mott Media, 1975.

Sally D. Reed, *NEA: Propaganda Front of the Radical Left*. Washington, D.C.: National Council for Better Education, 1984.

Ed Rowe, *New Age Globalism: Humanist Agenda for Building a New World Without God*. Herndon, Va.: Growth Publishing, 1985.

Those 10 books, the four quoted earlier, and several dozen more, infuriate their readers and add to the myths that surround public education. They also frequently serve as the catalyst that encourages people at the local level to challenge books, courses, and teaching methods. At least a half dozen of those books can be classified as best sellers, which underscores the fact that thousands of Americans are ready to buy and to read diatribes against the schools and their teachers.

Let's look again at the mythical school in your neighborhood. How is it perceived by the parents who read the books and newsletters of the critics, who listen to the televangelists denounce public education, and who join one of the hundreds of chapters of organizations that attack books, courses, and teaching methods?

Mythical Government Seminary 101 offers values clarification throughout the day so that students "will reject home-taught values." Students take sex-education courses that thrill them with "X-rated movies." Courses in drug education "teach them how to use drugs in a responsible manner" and intensify "their desire to experiment with drugs." They are taught by "left-leaning humanistic teachers" who are more interested in the goals of the NEA than in educating children.[7] They are brainwashed by the "educrats" in the religions of secular humanism, globalism, and New Age from the time they enter kindergarten. According to Tim LaHaye, atheistic brainwashing begins early in school with the look-say reading method.

"Progressive" (socialist) educators favored look-and-say teaching techniques. In the twenties they looked upon phonics as an enemy that must be replaced. To them, look-and-say was a theory based on their atheistic, humanistic beliefs and was a potent vehicle for indoctrinating (brainwashing) a whole generation of children's thinking. First, they made teachers of phonics seem archaic so that they could be replaced with the new look-and-say teachers, who, with their modern reading techniques, had also been heavily indoctrinated at Columbia University and other such schools with a socialist world view. In addition, they wanted to get rid of those phonics textbooks because they were profamily, promorality, pro-American, and prowork ethic and free enterprise.[8]

According to critics like Schlafly and LaHaye, phonics has virtually disappeared from reading textbooks. LaHaye even sees the lack of phonics instruction as part of a humanist conspiracy to lower the literacy level in the United States so that the Soviet Union can catch up. LaHaye notes that he does not know "if the conspiracy theory has any validity. I am aware, however, that John Dewey, the father of progressive education (which turned out to be regressive education and set the American school system back at least two decades), was a committed world socialist. . . . We should also note that while our educators have used the inferior look-and-say method of teaching reading and have raised the grades of our children to cover their falling scores, Russia is still using phonics. As our learning requirements and standards have dropped, Russia's have risen."[9]

LaHaye's frequently unsubstantiated charges are spread throughout the nation by a network of organizations that have grown almost exponentially in the last 15 years. (Among groups that sound the LaHaye alarm is Concerned Women of America, a very large and growing organization founded by Beverly LaHaye.) Shortly after I began studying the schoolbook protest movement 17 years ago, I wrote that I could name 200 organizations at the state, local, and national levels that attack public school textbooks, courses, and teaching methods. By 1985, I wrote that I was convinced that there are at least 2,000 such organizations. Why do I think so? Because some of the organizations named below have several hundred affiliates. Not all of those named below have state or local chapters; some, like Educational Research Analysts, have devoted followers who frequently act alone or in concert with other organizations at the local level.

American Education Association
American Education Coalition
America's Future, Inc.
The John Birch Society
Christian Anti-Communism Crusade
Citizens for Educational Freedom
Citizens for Excellence in Education
Citizens for Educational Reform
Concerned Women of America
Daughters of the American Revolution
Educational Research Analysts
Educational Voucher Institute
The Eagle Forum (Phyllis Schlafly)
Growing without Schooling
The Heritage Foundation

The Ku Klux Klan
National Association of Christian Educators
National Christian Action Coalition
National Congress for Educational Excellence
Posse Comitatus
Pro-family Forum
Save Our Schools
The 700 Club

During the 17 years that I have studied the schoolbook protest movement, I have read about the rise—and sometimes the fall—of hundreds of organizations at the local level. Some are formed as a direct spin-off of a state or national organization; others spring up because a group of parents become upset about something in a school. Some grow to become influential in a community; others die aborning; still others change their names and their affiliations several times either before they become a force in the community or before they dissolve. But regardless of their fate, organizations that precipitate, or participate in, schoolbook protests are becoming increasingly visible, vocal, and powerful.

An example of a large local group is Citizens for Better Education in the Plymouth-Canton (Michigan) school district. Advocating a return to Christian values in the schools, the 2,600-member organization succeeded in electing one school board member and tried—but failed—with a second candidate. The group's leader has attacked the use of the local newspaper in the classroom, "X-rated" movies, satanism, and the occult. The organization's goals and tactics are similar to those of Citizens for Excellence in Education, a national organization with an ever-increasing number of local chapters that wants to restore Christianity to the schools.

What in the public schools angers individuals and organizations? It is tempting to say everything, for in my 17 year study I have discovered that nearly every aspect of public education has incurred the wrath of some individual or group. Very early in my study, I reported 25 targets of the schoolbook protesters. A year later I raised the number to 40. Today I can list more than 200. But here are only 50.

1. Critical thinking skills.
2. Autobiography assignments, log books, diaries, and personal journals.
3. Programs that promote self-esteem.
4. Basal readers that do not champion phonics only.

15

5. Basal readers or any other textbooks that contain stories, poems, and plays that seem to favor disarmament, gun control, and pacifism.

6. Basal readers or any other textbooks containing stories, poems, and plays tht seem to be favorable toward feminism and/or the Equal Rights Amendment.

7. Basal readers or any other textbooks containing stories in which children make their own decisions, seem to be wiser than some adults, or can take care of most of their own needs.

8. Basal readers or any other textbooks containing stories, poems, or plays in which children question rules and decisions of adults.

9. Novels, stories, poems, or plays that portray conflicts between children and their parents or between children and persons in authority.

10. Stories about, or discussions of, the supernatural, the occult, magic, witchcraft, Halloween, etc.

11. Literary works that contain profanity or "questionable" language.

12. Literary works containing characters who cheat, lie, or steal. It is alleged that such characters are in the works to teach children how to cheat, lie, or steal.

13. Literary works containing characters who do not speak standard English. Such characters, it is alleged, are designed by the authors to teach students "bad English."

14. Black literature and black dialect.

15. Literary works and textbooks that portray women in nontraditional roles (anything other than housewife and mother). On the other hand, some feminist groups object to illustrations in basal readers and other textbooks that show women in the so-called traditional roles.

16. Mythology—particularly if the myths include stories of creation.

17. Organic evolution, including the idea that man has developed from previous or lower types of living things.

18. Scientific inquiry.

19. Stories about any pagan cultures and lifestyles.

20. The humanities. Several organizations have objected to the humanities because they "are part of the religion of secular humanism." The groups also reject "humanistic education" for the same reason.

21. Literature written by homosexuals; literature written about homosexuals; any favorable treatment of homosexuals.

22. Books and stories that do not champion the work ethic.

23. Books and stories that do not promote patriotism.

24. Negative statements about parents, about persons in authority, about the United States, about American traditions.

25. Science fiction.

26. Works of "questionable writers." Writers so labeled include Langston Hughes, Dick Gregory, Richard Wright, Malcolm X, Eldridge Cleaver, Joan Baez, and Ogden Nash.

27. "Trash." Examples: *The Catcher in the Rye, Go Ask Alice, Flowers for Algernon, Black Boy, Native Son, Manchild in the Promised Land, The Learning Tree, Black Like Me, Daddy Was a Numbers Runner,* and *Soul on Ice.*

28. Any books or stories that do not portray the family unit as the basis of American life.

29. Books and stories that are perceived to be unfavorable to Blacks. On the other hand, some individuals and groups have protested such books as *To Kill a Mockingbird* because they are "favorable to Blacks."

30. The use of masculine pronouns to refer to both male and female.

31. News stories that publish stories about the harsh realities of life—war, crime, death, violence, and sex.

32. Magazines that contain advertisements for alcoholic beverages, birth control devices, or trips to countries such as Cuba.

33. Nudity. Examples: the little boy in Maurice Sendak's *In the Night Kitchen* and reproductions of paintings showing half-clad gods and goddesses.

34. The swimwear issue of *Sports Illustrated.*

35. Depressing thoughts and negative statements about anything.

36. Education in human sexuality, including any mention of premarital sex, extramarital sex, contraception, abortion, homosexuality, group sex and marriage, prostitution, incest, masturbation, bestiality, divorce, population control, and roles of males and females.

37. Discussions of, or surveys of attitudes toward sex by students and/or their families.

38. Values clarification.

39. Use of moral dilemmas.

40. Discussion of religious or moral standards; role playing or open-ended discussions of situations involving moral issues.

41. Survival games, including life/death decision exercises.

42. Courses on drug and alcohol abuse.

43. Prevention guidance programs, especially those that include "contrived incidents for self-revelation; sensitivity training, group encounter sessions, talk-ins, magic circle techniques, self-evaluation and auto-criticism; strategies designed for self-disclosure (e.g., zig-zag)." (From a form letter prepared by the Maryland Coalition of Concerned Parents on Privacy Rights in the public schools and included in *Child Abuse in the Classroom.*)

44. "Death education, including any favorable mention of abortion, euthanasia, suicide, use of violence, and discussions of death and dying." (See number 43.)

45. "Anti-nationalistic, one-world government or globalism curriculum." (See number 43.)

46. World geography, if there is mention of "one worldism."

47. Histories that mention the United Nations, that refer to this country as a democracy instead of as a republic, that point out weaknesses in the founders of this nation or in any of the nation's leaders.

48. Human development and family development programs usually taught in home economics classes.

49. Invasions of privacy. Any quesitons, theme assignments, or homework that asks students to examine their personal backgrounds—family, education, religion, childhood experiences, etc.

50. Any psychological or psychiatric method practiced in the public schools. Any psychological principle used in teaching.

Teachers and administrators need to be aware of the major objections of the schoolbook protesters, not to get rid of the materials but in order to be prepared for attacks. When an organization is successful in removing a book, course, or teaching method in one school system, other chapters of the organization are likely to try to eliminate the same material elsewhere. Frequently, the second chapter will use exactly the same objections and tactics. And when an organization succeeds in banning one book or course, it is likely to try again for other items on its agenda.

It must be noted that there is nothing illegal about an organization's trying to remove materials from public schools. Therefore, it is imperative that school systems adopt comprehensive materials selection policies and procedures for handling complaints (see pages 93–98).

The recent decision in *Virgil v. School Board of Columbia County, Florida* 862 F.2d 1517 (11th Cir. 1989) underscores the need for procedures for handling complaints. In that case, the school board removed a humanities textbook from the high school because it contained Chaucer's "Miller's Tale" and Aristophanes's *Lysistrata*. After a parent com-

18

plained about the two classics, the school board adopted a Policy on Challenged State Adopted Textbooks to address any complaints regarding books in use in the curriculum. An advisory committee recommended that the textbook be retained in the curriculum but that the two "objectionable" works not be assigned as required reading. The superintendent disagreed with the committee's recommendation and recommended that the two disputed selections be deleted from the text or that the use of the book itself be terminated. The school board voted to discontinue any further use of the text.

Although both the trial and circuit courts disagreed with the board's reasons for removing the text, the circuit court decided that the board's removal of the classics on the basis of sexuality and vulgarity was not unconstitutional. The court noted that the board's action was reasonably related to a stated legitimate concern in light of the age of the students and the fact that the disputed materials were not banned from the school altogether.

The circuit court applied the *Hazelwood* standard to *Virgil*. The court noted that the board's decisions were curricular in nature, that the public "might reasonably perceive [the objectionable material] to bear the imprimatur of the school," and the board's removal was related to the "explicit sexuality and excessively vulgar language in the selections. It is clear from *Hazelwood* and other cases that this is a legitimate concern."

Given the *Virgil* and *Hazelwood* decisions and given the activities of organizations such as Citizens for Excellence in Education that declare their intention to elect their members to every school board, teachers, administrators, and librarians must be vigilant. They must insist that every school board have a comprehensive materials selection policy and procedures for handling complaints. And those procedures must prohibit anyone within a school system from acting unilaterally to remove anything from a school. Nothing should be removed until it is properly reviewed by a duly authorized reconsideration committee that gives its recommendations to the school board for action. Teachers, administrators, and librarians must also insist that everyone in a school corporation follow the procedures to the letter.

NOTES

1. Barbara M. Morris, *Change Agents in the School.* (Upland, Calif.: The Barbara M. Morris Report, 1979), p. 15.

2. Ibid.

3. Tim LaHaye, *The Battle for the Public School.* (Old Tappan, N.J.: Fleming H. Revell, 1983), p. 13.

4. Ibid., p. 14.

5. Erica Carle, *The Hate Factory.* (Milwaukee: Erica Carle Foundation, 1972), pp. 3–4.

6. The quotations are taken from a variety of organizations and authors critical of the public schools.

7. LaHaye, p. 44.

8. Ibid., pp. 46–47.

2. THE SIGNIFICANCE OF AND RATIONALE FOR ACADEMIC FREEDOM

by Jack L. Nelson, Graduate School of Education, Rutgers University

There are some principles that are so self-evident that there is no apparent need to restate them. That teachers in America should nourish the concept of freedom is an example. However, its restatement is important because the principle is not self-evident in the daily lives of teachers and students. Furthermore, traditions and practices that should follow from the principle of educational freedom in a democracy are poorly developed in public education, are virtually unexpressed in teacher education, and are under continuous and increasing threat from censorship and political restraint. Political restraint includes not only the effort to keep teachers and students from dealing with controversial topics, it also includes the constraints that result from statewide testing, atomistic performance objectives, accountability systems, and mandates curricula and texts. As Michael Apple and Kenneth Teitelbaum (1985) have eloquently stated, teachers have been "de-professionalized" by such practices that deny teachers freedom.

Academic freedom is the most significant concept teachers can embrace. The freedom to study, learn, teach, and express ideas is the defining characteristic of the concept of academic freedom for teachers and students. A society that intends to be free requires teachers who are willing and able to exercise academic freedom and provides a strong supportive climate for it. Unfortunately, a history of excessive restrictions on teacher and student freedom and a contemporary environment of imposed restraints on teachers in many locations illustrate the continuing threats to this most fragile, yet most important of professional concepts.

Howard Mumford Jones (1959), in his discussion of the American heritage from German universities, identifies academic freedom as incorporating two complementary elements—freedom of learning and freedom of teaching. He argues that tenure following a probationary period during which the teacher's competence is determined, is the strongest bulwark in defense of academic freedom. And Jones further recognizes that teachers below the college level in the United States have not enjoyed the kind of "community" respect the teacher enjoys in other countries, with the result that such teachers have been more restricted by local boards and administrators and have been "less well organized and less vigorous" in their defense of academic freedom (p. 229).

21

In the 30 years since Howard Mumford Jones made that statement, teachers have won and lost some academic freedom battles. However, the war over ideas has not been resolved in the favor of teachers and students. So long as teachers remain docile and "less vigorous" than they should be in their defense of academic freedom, the censorious and doctrinaire elements of society have unbridled opportunity to stifle dissent and de-professionalize teachers. This is an issue that needs to be continually addressed and readdressed by educators. There is a persistent professional obligation to defend and enhance academic freedom in the interest of a free society.

PROFESSIONAL SIGNIFICANCE OF ACADEMIC FREEDOM

Academic freedom is the central focus of the teaching profession. Professions can be defined by several characteristics, including (1) a required period of formal education, (2) specialized knowledge and skills, (3) a level of autonomy and responsibility in professional decisions, and (4) a shared commitment related to civilizing values pertinent to the practice of that profession. A required period of education is becoming commonplace for all occupations, but the professions have considerably increased the amount of that education. The professions of law and medicine have increased educational requirements since the beginning of the 20th century, from minimal academic work and short technical courses or self-study to current requirements involving formal schooling several years beyond undergraduate-level work. Teaching certification in most states has also increased in educational requirements during this century, moving from a semester's study in high school to minimum requirements of four- or five-year collegiate programs. Specialized knowledge and skills are essential in professions, law and medicine having evolved their own principles, language, and techniques of practice. Teaching has not developed as extensively, but has a defined body of accepted practice and principles.

Autonomy and responsibility in professional decisions have been accepted conditions of work for lawyers and medical doctors, with some exceptions, while teachers have suffered seriously in this aspect of being professional. As a result of legislative and administrative treatment of schools, teacher autonomy has never been strong in the United States. However, the free exercise of academic decision making demands teacher freedom. Academic decision making should include the capacity to influence the academic environment of the school, decisions on curriculum, selection of teacher materials and pedagogy, selection and review of school administrators, and evaluation of colleagues. These decisions require academic freedom, which incorporates autonomy and the acceptance of responsibility by teachers. It is significant that long-term control of schools by state and local boards and administrators has produced extraordinary systems of accountability that have actually reduced teacher autonomy and, thus, have reduced academic freedom.

A shared commitment to civilizing values, or social improvement, is also fundamental to a profession. In the legal profession, that commitment is to justice and jurisprudence, conveyed in the lawyer's code of ethics. In medicine, there is a commitment to healing, represented by the Hippocratic oath taken by students receiving their medical degree.

Despite the fact that some individual teachers, and some school boards and administrators, deny academic freedom by censorship and threat, there still remains a basic educational commitment to enlightenment. It is in the pursuit of this commitment that the teaching profession is obligated to continuing vigilance and expansion regarding academic freedom. This puts academic freedom at the center of the profession, a matter of extraordinary significance. It is, therefore, a matter of profound concern for the teaching profession to develop the idea that academic freedom is basic to the survival of the profession and to the democratic society that it serves.

The National Education Association's Code of Ethics for Teachers addresses academic freedom in Principle 4. The American Federation of Teachers includes academic freedom as one of its prime goals. Many professional associations of subject field teachers have been very active in efforts to protect academic freedom; most obvious have been the National Council of Teachers of English and the National Council for the Social Studies. The American Association of University Professors recently emphasized the responsibility of colleges and university faculty for protecting precollegiate teacher freedoms (AAUP 1986) and has presented Amicus briefs in support of classroom teachers in court cases. The American Civil Liberties Union has repeatedly published documents in support of academic freedom and has provided legal assistance to teachers who are challenged in court cases. The American Library Association regularly publishes cases of restrictions on teachers in its *Intellectual Freedom Newsletter*. People for the American Way publishes an informative, though depressing, annual report on censorship that shows the extent of controversies threatening academic freedom. Similar reports on censorship are presented regularly by the British *Index on Censorship* and by Project Censored, which identifies the 10 most-censored news stories each year.

Despite the apparent interest of these and other organizations in protecting teacher freedom and exposing efforts to restrict it, academic freedom remains a fragile and elusive concept that is often abrogated by school officials, special interest organizations, and teachers themselves by compliance and self-censorship. John Jones (1966) stated it clearly: "One of the lesser known and understood freedoms in America is that of academic freedom, and consequently it is perhaps one that is most frequently violated" (p.7). Academic freedom needs continuing vigilance to prevent its erosion.

Upton Sinclair (1924), who spent two years visiting schools across the United States and found myriad examples of censorship, restriction, and threat, stated these pithy comments:

> The present status of the American school teacher is that of a wage-slave, an employee of the school board and the superintendent; it is not the status of a free citizen, nor of a professional expert . . . It is necessary both for the schools and for the children, that teachers should cease to be rabbits, and should become self-respecting and alert citizens. (pp. 405, 407)

Unfortunately, although several conditions for teachers have improved in the years since Sinclair studied schools, inappropriate restraints on teacher and student freedom continue. There is evidence that censorship of schools has actually increased in the past 10 years, with a tripling of reported incidents since 1970 (Jenkinson 1985; Carlson 1987; People for the American Way 1988). And academic freedom seems no more secure now, without teacher vigilance, than it was 50 years ago (Nelson and Stanley 1985; Nelson and Ochoa 1987).

SOCIAL SIGNIFICANCE OF ACADEMIC FREEDOM

We need to regularly rethink the fundamental grounding of academic freedom in the nature of the society as well as in the schools and the profession. Teaching in a totalitarian society can itself be totalitarian, or without thought, or dangerous to the teacher. Totalitarian teaching in a democracy is not only illogical, it is dangerous to the concept of democracy. Thoughtless teaching in a democracy is also dangerous—to the society and to the profession of teaching. The social cost of avoiding controversy and accepting censorship and control is too great a price for students and society to pay for short-term conformity. It puts the concept of democracy in peril.

John Dewey phrased it succinctly over one-half century ago: "Since freedom of mind and freedom of expression are the root of all freedom, to deny freedom in education is a crime against democracy" (Dewey 1936, p. 136). Dewey, one of the founders of the AAUP as an organization to protect academic freedom for college teachers, maintained a strong commitment to similar freedoms for K–12 teachers.

The U.S. Supreme Court, in a 1967 decision that found a state-mandated loyalty oath for college teachers to be unconstitutional, noted the importance of academic freedom to the society:

Our nation is deeply committed to safeguarding academic freedom which is of transcendent value to all of us and not merely to the teachers concerned. That freedom is, therefore, a special concern of the First Amendment, which does not tolerate laws that cast a pall of orthodoxy over the classroom . . . The classroom is peculiarly the "marketplace of ideas." *(Keyishian v. Board of Regents,* 1967).

Although the details of the *Keyishian* case involved college teachers, the principle remains for teachers at the K–12 level. However, teachers at the elementary and secondary levels have been less obvious in their claims and demands for academic freedom than have been their counterparts at the college level. However, school teachers deserve similar protections for academic freedom grounded on the same rationale presented in the *Keyishian* case for a democratic society. Alexander Mieklejohn, former president of Amherst College and national leader in the protection of academic freedom for college professors, commented in *Harper's Magazine* in 1938 that school teachers "must discuss controversial questions. There is no other program by which the education of a free people will be carried on" (Mieklejohn 1938, p. 20). Noted historian Howard K. Beale, after a two-year study investigating and documenting the excessive restrictions on teacher freedom, remarked: "freedom in teaching is important not because it is a right of the teacher but because it is essential to an intelligent solution of the problems of modern society" (Beale 1936, p. 615). And the American Civil Liberties Union phrased the relationship between the school and a free society, "A school which does not respect civil liberties has failed the community, its students, and itself" (*Academic Freedom in the Secondary School*, 1968, p. 20).

Democracy, in the Jeffersonian tradition, is singularly dependent upon an enlightened people involved in self-governance. Free education and freedom in education are necessary conditions to that civilizing enterprise of democracy. Bertrand Russell notes that without universal education, "democracy cannot exist except as an empty form" (Russell 1928, p. 128). While Russell properly chastises government-operated schools for teaching docility, undue respect for existing institutions and authority, and avoidance of all fundamental criticism of the society, he identifies the teacher as "by far the best of the forces concerned in education, and it is primarily to him or her that we must look for progress" (p. 129).

The link of the teacher to democracy is also expressed by Henry Giroux, in an article in the May 1985 issue of *Social Education*, where he states the principle that teachers must be "transformative intellectuals," committed to exercising their calling in the free exchange of ideas and in the regaining of positions of power in school decisions. The purpose for that empowerment is to increase individual freedom and social justice, consistent with democracy where critical examination of issues is essential. This is at the heart of education in a society that attempts to be an open democracy. Academic freedom is a necessity in this endeavor and teachers should be at the forefront of this movement.

TEACHER COMPETENCE NECESSARY FOR ACADEMIC FREEDOM

Academic freedom is not simply license to do what one wishes without restraint. No freedom is absolute; all have commensurate responsibilities. In academic freedom the prime responsibility is professional competence. Competence in teaching may be complex and difficult to measure, but it is the necessary condition to assure academic freedom. That competence is more than the sum of knowledge of subject matter and pedagogy; it is a reasoned commitment to student and teacher freedom. Teachers are evaluated continually during their professional preparation as well as during their probationary period. The result of this process is the determination of whether to grant tenure. Teacher tenure should not be seen merely as job security. Rather, its significance is in the need to protect teachers from political interference in the performance of their duties and to ensure a stable and free teacher corps.

Tenure is not the only requisite for academic freedom. College students preparing to be teachers and probationary period teachers also deserve protection and access to due process to determine whether they have acted in a competent manner in a particular situation. But tenure serves as the major protection against the political pressures and censorship that threaten academic freedom. It is to the tenured teachers that one must look to provide leadership in assuring academic freedom and due process for nontenured teachers and for students. If the sphere of academic freedom is to be broadened, tenured teachers must understand this leadership role to be a major part of the acceptance of tenure in the profession.

SOME PROBLEMS IN ACADEMIC FREEDOM

Academic freedom is a fragile concept in the United States. Our society, to the extent that it is free and open, is susceptible to platitudes and slogans. On the one hand, that is among the several charms of modern America; advertising jingles and 30-second-long sound bites fit with the yuppie concept of being high on technology and short on thought. Certainly, the short focus on substance fits with the increased pace of life in technology and communication. On the other hand, it presents a serious problem in education, a problem not extensively examined in the cur-

26

rent educational reform literature. There is little in current media treatments of social issues and human problems that appears to have been subjected to the search in analysis and deep inquiry skills that we educators are supposed to have been developing in our students for these past 50 years. Among the victims of high technology is critical thinking.

The public susceptibility to propaganda and its willingness to return to an era of red baiting, McCarthy-like attacks on intellectual freedom, and censorship of ideas that are outside of the mainstream represent significant threats to academic freedom for teachers and students. These threats are in the form of public policies that restrain teachers and students, of increased intrusion into the schools and classrooms, and increasing teacher fear and self-censorship in a quest for survival. Educators have a social and professional responsibility to educate the society to the need for academic freedom. This is an area where much more work is required. Schools are appropriate places to provide that education for each generation. Academic freedom and censorship are suitable topics for discussion in courses in English, the arts, science, social studies, and others where the problems have been most evident. We need new generations of the public, elected officials, business and labor leaders, school board members, and parents who understand the necessity for intellectual freedom and can assist in its defense for schools.

Among the problems facing academic freedom are teacher education programs that ignore attention to the concept of academic freedom. Teacher certification requirements do not mention it and very few teacher education textbooks treat the subject. And, most unfortunately, prospective teachers are often put in student teaching situations where they learn that teachers are supposed to avoid controversy and accept restrictions (Palonsky and Nelson 1980). The result is that many teachers have not had the opportunity to study academic freedom, to understand its importance, and to recognize their professional obligations in regard to it. The professional socialization of teachers typically disregards academic freedom as being at the core of the profession.

A further problem related to academic freedom is the sterilization of the curriculum, which blocks student exercise of freedom. Teaching that avoids controversy, resorts to memorization and drill, and that trivializes knowledge by making it dull and "testable" is not education. While it is possible to teach a set of what Alfred North Whitehead called "inert ideas" (Whitehead 1929), no credible teacher or other educational authority has seriously proposed that approach. Despite the considerable, and appropriate, disputation over what schooling should be, there is no evident group of educators that advocates rote memorization and simple indoctrination of boring and sterile material as the purpose of education. Yet, schools engage in these sterilizing activities to avoid controversy and

27

academic
freedom = freedom of speech,
no censorship(?)

to meet test-based accountability requirements.

Another problem regarding academic freedom is found in conflicting legal precedents that cause confusion for teachers and schools. There is a scatter of state court decisions, some of which seem to limit teacher and student freedom in the determination of curriculum, and there are others which support those freedoms in regard to teaching materials and methods (O'Neil 1981; Stewart 1989). At the U.S. Supreme Court level, the *Keyishian* decision (1967), is important in supporting academic freedom, and the *Tinker* decision (1969) extended citizen rights including free expression to students. Recent decisions, however, appear to limit academic freedom by allowing limited rights of school boards to censor books (*Board of Education, Island Trees Union Free School District No. 26 v. Pico* 1982), allowing restrictions to be imposed on student free speech (*Bethel School District v. Fraser* 1986), and allowing school officials to censor school newspapers (*Hazelwood School District v. Kuhlmeier* 1988). The issues posed in these cases are excellent teaching material; however, most important, they provide evidence of conflicting interpretations that result in the current state of confusion. This is an opportune time for educators to undertake a massive effort at public education to establish the social and professional necessity of strong conditions of support for academic freedom.

NEEDED IMPROVEMENTS
IN ACADEMIC FREEDOM IN AMERICA

The case for academic freedom needs to be reconsidered in each era. Those who would read a treatise on academic freedom are likely to be convinced of the necessity for free inquiry, but there is a need to reidentify with others who share the professional commitment to enlightenment. This involves a rejuvenation of our core educational values, and preparation for battles over this important terrain. We have often been surprised because we do not have a very effective early warning system to detect the next assault on educational freedom. We may be too late already for early warning in the current skirmish.

Our professional journals do not regularly carry news of censorship and academic freedom concerns; thus, teachers are often unaware until the problem has become a public issue. The extensive efforts of concerned groups at exposing censorship and advancing teacher and student freedom are usually ignored in the education journals. Organizations that are devoted to keeping teachers informed include the Intellectual Freedom Committee of the American Library Association, the National Coalition Against Censorship, the *Index on Censorship*, People for the American Way, the ACLU, and Project Censored at Sonoma State Uni-

28

Academic freedom is a core value for a democratic society

versity. Clearly, we need still better communication.

The profession would be substantially strengthened by the publication of a teacher handbook on academic freedom and censorship, by scholarly publications on this topic, and by conferences sponsored by professional associations to elaborate and reinforce the concept. Since the 1930s there has been insufficient attention or research and scholarship on academic freedom in schools.

Expanded networking efforts are needed to provide teachers with legal counseling and financial support to fight intrusions on their freedom. Teacher educators need to include study of academic freedom in teacher education programs, and to have academic freedom among the ideas examined in the schools. In a society where censorship and political restraints are continuing problems, schools should provide for examination of such matters and their consequences for a democracy. Such study may be controversial, but that only defines it as education.

Further, the profession would benefit by establishing national awards for teachers who have struggled to protect academic freedom. Such action has already been taken by the National Council for Social Studies, among others. We also need to establish widely recognized and respected commissions to investigate and report on the current state of affairs regarding censorship and academic freedom.

Teacher associations can help by collective efforts to define standards of conduct for academic freedom. They can also investigate allegations of serious infringement on academic freedom, with resultant public censuring if required. This is already a tradition for the AAUP for college-level cases and they have experienced considerable success in protecting academic freedom. Finally, all educators need to become more persuasive in influencing legislation toward increasing teacher and student freedoms and expanding teacher autonomy.

The significance of, and rationale for, academic freedom places it as the central principle for the profession of teaching. Furthermore, it is a core value for a democratic society. There is no better time than now to rethink the social and professional nature of academic freedom, to assert its centrality to a free society and strengthening American education, and to develop new practices that reject the tradition of stultification, sterilization, and de-professionalization in American schools.

REFERENCES

American Association of University Professors. *Liberty and Learning in the Schools.* Washington, D.C.: AAUP, 1986.
American Civil Liberties Union. *Academic Freedom in the Secondary*

Schools. New York: ACLU, 1968.

Apple, Michael, and Teitelbaum, Kenneth. "Deskilling Teachers." *Social Education* 49 (1985): 372–75.

Beale, Howard. *Are American Teachers Free?* New York: Scribner's, 1936.

Bethel School District No. 403 v. Fraser, 106 Sup. Ct. 3159 (1986).

Board of Education, Island Trees Union Free School District v. Pico, 457 U.S. 853 (1982).

Carlson, Ken. "Academic Freedom in Hard Times." *Social Education* 51 (1987): 429–30.

Dewey, John. "The Social Significance of Academic Freedom." *Social Frontier* 2 (1936): 136.

Giroux, Henry. "The Teacher as Transformative Intellectual." *Social Education* 49 (1985): 376–79.

Hazelwood School District v. Kuhlmeier. 33 U.S. 299 (1988).

Jenkinson, E. B. "Protecting Holden Caulfield and His Friends from the Censors." *English Journal* 45 (1985): 28.

Jones, Howard Mumford. "The American Concept of Academic Freedom." In *Academic Freedom and Tenure*, edited by Louis Joughlin. Washington, D.C.: AAUP, 1959.

Jones, John M., Jr. *Academic Freedom and the Secondary School Teacher and Other Heretical Essays on Education.* Philadelphia: G. H. Buchanan Press, 1966.

Keyishian v. Board of Regents. 385 U.S. 589 (1987).

Mieklejohn, Alexander. "Teachers and Controversial Questions." *Harper's* 177 (1938): 15–22.

Nelson, Jack L., and Ochoa, Anna. "Academic Freedom, Censorship and the Social Studies." *Social Education* 51 (1987): 424–27.

Nelson, Jack L., and Stanley, William. "Academic Freedom in Social Education: Fifty Years Standing Still." *Social Education* 49 (1985): 662–64.

O'Neil, Robert M. *Classrooms in the Crossfire.* Bloomington, Ind.: University of Indiana Press, 1981.

Palonsky, Stuart, and Nelson, Jack L. "Political Restraint in the Socialization of Student Teachers." *Theory and Research in Social Education* 7 (1980): 19–34.

People for the American Way. *Attacks on the Freedom to Learn, 1987–1988.* Sixth Annual Survey. Washington, D.C.: People for the American Way, 1980.

Russell, Bertrand. *Sceptical Essays.* London: George Allen and Unwin, 1928.

Sinclair, Upton. *The Goslings.* Pasadena: Sinclair, 1924.

Stewart, Malcolm. "The First Amendment, the Public Schools and the Inculcation of Community Values." *Journal of Law and Education* 18 (1989): 23–92.

Tinker v. Des Moines Independent School District. 393 U.S. 503, 571 (1969).

Whitehead, A. N. *The Aims of Education.* London: Collier Macmillan, 1929.

3. ACADEMIC FREEDOM: WHAT THE COURTS HAVE SAID

by John L. Strope, Jr., Professor, University of South Alabama;
and Cathy Broadwell, Curriculum and Research Division,
Mobile County Public Schools

Throughout this book, numerous definitions of academic freedom have been provided. From a realistic viewpoint, those definitions are really only an intellectual exercise. What matters is what the courts, especially the Supreme Court, have said about academic freedom. In 1957, the Court said:

> No one should underestimate the vital role in a democracy that is played by those who guide and train our youth. To impose any straightjacket upon the intellectual leaders in our colleges and universities would imperil the future of our Nation. No field of education is so thoroughly comprehended by man that new discoveries cannot yet be made. . . . Scholarship cannot flourish in an atmosphere of suspicion and distrust. Teachers and students must always remain free to inquire, to study and to evaluate, to gain new maturity and understanding; otherwise our civilization will stagnate and die.[1]

Again in 1967, the Supreme Court said:

> Our Nation is deeply committed to safeguarding academic freedom, which is of transcendent value to all of us and not merely to the teachers concerned. That freedom is therefore a special concern of the First Amendment, which does not tolerate laws that cast a pall of orthodoxy over the classroom. The classroom is peculiarly the "marketplace of ideas." The Nation's future depends upon leaders trained through wide exposure to that robust exchange of ideas which discovers truth out of a multitude of tongues [rather] than through any kind of authoritative selection.[2]

Finally, in 1960, the Court said:

> The vigilant protection of constitutional freedoms is nowhere more vital than in the community of American schools. By limiting the power of the States to interfere with freedom of speech and freedom of inquiry and freedom of association, the Fourteenth Amendment protects all persons no matter what their calling. But, in view of the nature of the teacher's relation to the effective exercise of the rights which are safeguarded by the Bill of Rights and by the Fourteenth Amendment, inhibition of freedom of thought, and of action upon thought, in the case of teachers brings the safeguards of those amendments vividly into operation. Such unwarranted inhibition upon the free spirit of teachers has an unmistakable tendency to kill that free play of the spirit which all teachers ought especially to cultivate and practice. . . .[3]

How useful are these cases for those who claim academic freedom and who work in public school settings in this country? Unfortunately, the first two cases from which we have quoted involved controversies that arose in higher education during the McCarthy era and in the years immediately thereafter. The last case involved a requirement that a public school teacher identify organizations to which he belonged. Thus, none of the cases, while containing language that seems relevant, actually involved claims of academic freedom in the sense being considered here. Therefore, determining what the courts have said requires analysis of opinions from lower federal and state courts.

The major focus is upon the few cases where K–12 public school teachers went to court arguing for their right to academic freedom. While most of the cases include claims involving other constitutional or statutory rights, only the legal discussions and outcomes relating to academic freedom will be presented. Essentially the courts have been silent on issues of academic freedom during the '80s.

Some additional cases, though not necessarily brought by teachers and not necessarily argued on the basis of academic freedom, also will be described because they offer insights for understanding whatever rights that teachers have. Interestingly, these cases have received attention during the 1980s.

TEACHERS GO TO COURT

Course Content

Frances Ahern was a high school economics teacher in Grand Island, Nebraska.[4] She was ordered by her principal to cease teaching politics in her economics classes. Yvonne Adams, an English teacher in a Wyoming school district, was similarly ordered to stop discussing politics in her classes.[5] Two teachers from the state of Washington initiated a new approach to teaching history.[6] They, and other teachers, requested that a pilot Global Studies Program be instituted as an alternative to a more conventional history course. In 1973, the school district approved and implemented this pilot program.

Subsequently, however, students were given a choice between conventional history and Global Studies. A vast majority chose the more conventional course, which resulted in fewer Global Studies sections. During the 1976 spring semester, one of the two teachers, Millikan, was assigned to teach one conventional history class and four Global Studies classes. As a consequence of student preference, registration for the 1976 fall semester fell such that the Global Studies program was reduced to one class. Millikan was required to teach four regular history classes. His team

32

teaching partner, Robert Peterson, was transferred from his team teaching assignment with Millikan to another position in the school during the spring of 1976.

Ahern, Adams, Millikan, and Peterson claimed a violation of their academic freedom right to determine course content. In all of the cases, the courts took the position that a school district has authority to prescribe course content. The teachers lost in each case.

The *Millikan* court found that the course in Global Studies differed from the more conventional courses in coverage and content. The court concluded that since significant course content differences existed, and course content is manifestly a matter within the board's discretion, the teachers' claim of academic freedom must fail. The courts said: "While teachers should have some measure of freedom in teaching techniques employed, they may not ignore or omit essential course material or disregard the course calendar."

Required Materials

The classic case on this topic involves a high school English teacher from Massachusetts.[7] Robert Keefe wanted to expose his students to provocative, contemporary writing. He gave each member of his class a current issue of the *Atlantic Monthly* magazine, provided by the school system, and assigned the lead article, which discussed dissent, protest, and revolt. The article was entitled, "The Young and the Old," and it contained the term for "an incestuous son" in numerous places. Although there was no evidence of negative student reaction, a number of parents found the word offensive and protested to the school board. Members of the board asked Keefe if he would agree not to use the word again in class, but Keefe refused. Proceedings were then begun to terminate him.

In ruling for Keefe, the court concluded that the offending word was important to the article and that the article was relevant for the particular course. In addition, the court considered the age of the students—they were seniors—and their familiarity with such words and concepts. The court concluded that under the circumstances, the word probably did not shock the students. Finally, the court concluded that the sensibilities of the offended parents were not the "full measure of what is proper in education." Robert Keefe won.

Late in her first year of teaching, Marilyn Parducci was teaching her junior English classes about the short story.[8] She assigned an outside reading entitled "Welcome to the Monkey House," by Kurt Vonnegut. The next morning she was called to the principal's office, where the principal and an associate superintendent told her of phone calls from displeased parents and of their views of the trashiness of the story. Within days, she was officially terminated by the board of education.

Quoting approvingly from *Keefe*, the court found no evidence that the assignment was an inappropriate reading for high school juniors. In addition, the court looked to whether the assignment had created "a significant disruption to the educational processes of this school." The court could find no evidence of any significant disruption. The impact of the "significant disruption" standard today must be considered in view of *Hazelwood School District v. Kuhlmeier* (see pp. 44–45). Finally, the court looked at the question of prior notice that the conduct for which she was punished had been prohibited, a claim earlier made by Robert Keefe. In finding a lack of such notice, the court stated:

> Our laws in this country have long recognized that no person be punished for conduct unless such conduct has been proscribed in clear and precise terms. . . . When a teacher is forced to speculate as to what conduct is permissible and what conduct is proscribed, he is apt to be overly cautious and reserved in the classroom. Such a reluctance on the part of the teacher to investigate and experiment with new and different ideas is anathema to the entire concept of academic freedom.

When relevance to the course and appropriateness to the age and maturity of the students are considered, teachers do not always win. Clara Brubaker, John Brubaker, and Ronald Sievert were junior high teachers in Illinois.[9] Soon after seeing the movie, "Woodstock," the three teachers decided to distribute brochures that they had acquired at the theatre. Several parts of one poem in the brochure related to drugs and sexual behavior, and contained perceived vulgarities.

Mrs. Brubaker taught French, Mr. Brubaker taught industrial arts, and Mr. Sievert taught language arts. The court could find no educational purpose served by distributing such vulgar material to students in junior high school. The board's decision to terminate the teachers prior to the end of the school year was upheld.

Rex Fisher was a tenured teacher in Fairbanks, Alaska.[10] He taught a course in American minorities that included a unit on homosexual rights. Fisher chose to use a book entitled *The Front Runner* as supplemental reading for his students. The school district had a policy that required prior administrative approval for any supplementary teaching material. As soon as the principal determined that Fisher was using an unapproved book, he notified him in writing about this policy. Since Fisher persisted, the principal followed up with another memo and again reminded Fisher of the policy.

In both instances, Fisher was instructed directly not to use the book until it was approved. In the face of a direct violation of a reasonable policy, the teacher's claim of academic freedom failed. The court said: "The school board's authority over classroom material is very broad."

34

However, the court went on to indicate that a board's decision was not unfettered by the Constitution. For example, a board could not design a curriculum to favor a particular religion, or to force racial bias, or partisan political preference into the classroom.

In a similar case, several fellow teachers joined Bob Cary in bringing suit against the local board of education when it banned 10 books from a total of 1,285 titles submitted for use in language arts classes in local high schools.[11] The classes involved were elective courses for eleventh and twelfth grade students and were entitled "Contemporary Literature," "Contemporary Poetry," and "American Masters." Board policies allowed for teachers to choose reading materials from classroom libraries or personal sources. The books were not approved for purchase with school district funds nor could they be used for class assignments or for giving academic credit for reading any of the books.

The teachers argued that once the board had approved the courses, then the teachers had the right of academic freedom to use any nonobscene materials. The teachers did not argue for the board to purchase or endorse any books, and made it clear that students would not be required to read any particular book. The board argued that teachers could comment upon and recommend that students read the books. Teachers could meet with students anywhere outside of class to discuss any book. The books could even be discussed in the classroom so long as the discussion was not protracted as, in effect, to amount to using the nonselected book. The teachers lost.

After the promising results of *Keefe* and *Parducci*, and the rather obvious outcome in *Brubaker*, what happened to *Fisher* and *Cary*? The *Fisher* court knowingly rejected the logic in cases like *Keefe* and *Parducci*. The *Cary* court summed up its logic:

> It is legitimate for the curriculum of the school district to reflect the value system and educational emphasis that are the collective will of those children who are being educated and who are paying the cost.... If the board may decide that contemporary poetry may not be offered; if it may select the major text of the course; why may it not go further and exclude certain books from being assigned for instruction in the course?

Teaching Strategies

Claims of academic freedom in the use of teaching strategies, rather than course content or required materials, appear to be the most likely claim for teachers to win. Janet Cooper employed a technique known as the "Sunshine" simulation to teach post-Civil War U.S. history.[12] The technique involved role playing by students in order to recreate that period of history. It evoked strong student feelings on racial issues. Parental

35

complaints about Cooper increased significantly as a result of this project. Cooper was twice called before the principal to discuss the project. She was told not to discuss "blacks in American history" and that "nothing controversial should be discussed in the classroom." When decisions were made by the school board about which teachers to rehire for the following year, the board decided not to rehire Cooper. At trial, board members could find little to fault Cooper's teaching performance apart from the complaint they received about the Sunshine simulation. Both the principal and superintendent had recommended that her contract be renewed. Cooper was victorious.

As part of a civics class in a public high school in Texas, Keith Sterzing taught a six-day unit on race relations.[13] Several parents complained about the material used during this unit as well as about the true-false and multiple choice test covering the unit. In addition, these parents were upset at some of Mr. Sterzing's honest responses to some students' questions about interracial marriages. Sterzing expressed his lack of opposition to such marriages.

The court indicated: "A responsible teacher must have freedom to use the tools of his profession as he sees fit. If the teacher cannot be trusted to use them fairly, then the teacher should never have been engaged in the first place." The court concluded that Mr. Sterzing's objectives in his teaching were proper to stimulate critical thinking, did create an awareness of our present political and social community, and enlivened the educational process. To the court these were desirable objectives. Sterzing's termination was reversed.

In connection with teaching about sex roles in her psychology class, Ms. Dean introduced a survey published in *Psychology Today*.[14] The survey was entitled "Masculinity—What It Means to Be a Man," and dealt in part with the subject of sexual intercourse in an explicit fashion. Ms. Dean allowed a senior student who needed the opportunity to do some make-up work to administer the survey. The testimony indicated that Ms. Dean had not done a very thorough job of reading the article and the survey in their entirety, and had not given the student specifically concrete instructions to deal with this sensitive material. While there was no disruption or outburst in the classes, there was community reaction.

The unrest led to the board's terminating Ms. Dean. Since there was no evidence of disruption of the learning environment, the court concluded that Ms. Dean must win. The court addressed the school board's argument regarding community disruption:

No subject which differed from the majoritarian view would ever be taught in the public schools. Every scientific advancement was at one time a new idea, and most new ideas are controversial. The process of education has been described as the shedding of dogmas. There is comfort in the security of

36

old and familiar dogmas, and many times the cloak of morality and even righteousness becomes intertwined with familiar values, perceptions, and dogmas. To exclude a subject from the public school curriculum because it offends the community, or to discharge a teacher from objectively presenting that subject, runs counter to the spirit of the First Amendment, and posed a threat greater than the unsettling effect on the community precipitated by the student's intellectual exposure to matters that approach concepts long regarded as taboo.

Lest you begin to get the wrong idea and think that these academic freedom claims relating to teaching strategies are always winners, let us return to a couple of aspects of two cases that were mentioned earlier. Remember Frances Ahern, the economics teacher who taught politics in her classes? Well, she also changed her teaching strategies. She allowed students the choice of subjects for daily discussions, the choice of course materials, and the chance to establish rules for classroom behavior. She was instructed by her principal to return to more conventional teaching methods and to restore order promptly in her classes. To the court, these were valid dictates of her employer and her claim of academic freedom was unsuccessful.

Remember Millikan and Peterson who taught the course in Global Studies? These teachers wanted to continue team teaching the course in Global Studies. In addition, the course emphasized small groups, independent reading and writing, and inquiry. Thus, the opportunities for Millikan and Peterson to use the teaching strategies that they preferred were curtailed when the sections in Global Studies were all but eliminated. The school system had allowed the pilot program to be conducted and, according to the court, had assigned Millikan and Peterson to conventional sections only when pre-enrollment projections declined. There was no indication of any effort to deny these teachers their academic freedom over content or teaching strategies; this was just a practical management decision.

The Wyoming teacher, Yvonne Adams, was criticized for the informal seating arrangements in her classroom and for lack of discipline. In addition, she participated in conducting a book club for students every other week in the evening at her home or that of another teacher. The court quickly determined there was no violation of academic freedom as it said:

Undoubtedly, they have some freedom in the techniques to be employed, but this does not say that they have an unlimited liberty as to structure and content of the courses at least at the secondary level. Thus, in a small community like Gillette the Board members and the principal surely have a right to emphasize a more orthodox approach. . . .

Other teachers came to similar ends. Lloyd Dale, a biology teacher, was terminated because of his repeated unwillingness to diminish his focus on theories of creation and related religious ideas.[15] Another teacher, Phillip Burns, devised a letter-writing activity as part of a handwriting lesson for his fifth grade students[16] The letters were written to his fiancée who responded to each student with this or a similar statement:

> I am a communist, in the Progressive Labor Party, just like Phil [Burns] is. We are both working hard for the day when you kids and the rest of us working people kick out all the rich rotten bosses and then we can all run everything ourselves. That is what communism really means. Then we can all cooperate and have a good and happy life. My son, Chris, is learning to be a communist too!

A Wyoming teacher's involvement with an April Fool's Day issue of the school newspaper led to the board's displeasure.[17] As newspaper advisor, he permitted the publication of a picture of a row of urinals as well as letters to the editor and an article entitled, "Old Meany Master," which expressed "critical opinions of the disciplinary actions of certain teachers." In rejecting cases like *Parducci*, the court concluded that "academic freedom must be viewed as an interest of all society, but this does not mean that improper conduct can be condoned under the guise of such freedom."

Two fifth grade teachers lost their jobs in somewhat similar incidents.[18] Allen Celestine learned that two of his female students had been using vulgar language (the "f" word), so he required them to write the word one thousand times and to have the principal and their parents sign the paper. Another teacher, Mahalia Frison read a note to her students that had been written by another student in the class. The note contained "vulgar colloquialisms." Considering the age of the students and the lack of any educational purpose served by the punishment, the courts ruled against both teachers.

Speakers/Assemblies/Plays

While these activities may occur outside the classroom, they certainly relate to the "teaching job" of all teachers. Dean Wilson was a teacher of political science at a high school in Oregon.[19] Previously, he had invited a Democrat, a Republican, and a member of the John Birch Society to speak. When he invited a Communist to speak to the same class, he followed the same procedure of informing the principal, who approved this activity. The school board also approved the invitation, but after mixed reviews in the community, reversed its decision. In a decision supporting Wilson's claim, the court said:

> I am firmly convinced that a course designed to teach students that a free and democratic society is superior to those in which freedoms are sharply curtailed will fail entirely, if it fails to teach one important lesson—that the power of

the state is never so great that it can silence a man or woman simply because there are those who disagree.

The *Wilson* case was not an outcome that was inconsistent with other cases in the mid-1970s. However, where are we 15 years later? A Maine case with very similar-sounding facts offers the opposite result.[20] David Solmitz, a high school teacher, began planning an all-day "Symposium on Tolerance." Tolerance Day was designed to bring to the school representatives of many different groups who had experienced prejudice in society. When word got out into the community that the program would include a lesbian, the school board received extensive negative reaction. The reactions included bomb threats, threats of sabotage to the school's heating plant, and indications that parents would keep their children home or picket the school on Tolerance Day.

The school board decided to cancel the Tolerance Day program. However, the board did nothing to discipline the teacher; it did not tell him how to teach his history course; nor did it restrict him in any way from freely expressing his views on any subjects within or without the school. Neither did the board prohibit any other discussion of tolerance or prejudice against homosexuals. Under the circumstances, the court concluded that the board's action did not infringe on the academic freedom of the teacher.

The cases in this section offer further insight into understanding academic freedom. Some of these cases do not directly involve teachers and some of the cases make no reference whatsoever to academic freedom. However, each in its own way helps our understanding. Most significant of all is that most of these cases have occurred during the 1980s. They paint a distinctly different orientation by the courts than that evident in the 1970s.

Course Content

Louisiana parents and teachers challenged the "Balanced Treatment of Creation-Science and Evolution-Science in Public School Instruction Act," a state statute.[21] The Act forbade teaching the theory of evolution unless accompanied by instruction in "creation-science," and vice versa. Plaintiffs challenged this statute as a violation of the establishment clause of the First Amendment.

The state legislature expressed, as its purpose for passing the Act, the protection of academic freedom! Apparently, according to the court, members of the state legislature had defined academic freedom to mean teaching "all the evidence," assuring a basic fairness in talking about human development. The court read the legislative history of the statute as suggesting quite the opposite—legislators wanted neither concept to be taught or, at least, they opposed teaching the theory of evolution. Teachers were actually worse off after the state's passage because previously no law had forbade the teaching of any scientific theory. The effort to change the definition of academic freedom to fit a desired result could not save the statute from violating the establishment clause of the First Amendment. A statute whose basic purpose was to support a particular religious view cannot stand.

A related case is *Smith v. Board of School Commissioners*.[22] The case arose in Mobile, Alabama, where fundamentalist Christian parents objected to some 44 U.S. history and home economics textbooks. They claimed the books advanced the religion of secular humanism while inhibiting Christian religions. They wanted the books banned from public schools. The federal district judge's "burn-the-books-order" was reversed on appeal by the Court of Appeals for the Eleventh Circuit. The parents had claimed that these books taught students to make their own decisions, to use the scientific method, and to think for themselves. This, they claimed, worked to the advantage of secular humanism and to the disadvantage of Christianity. The Court of Appeals agreed with the parents' characterization of the books. Indeed, the books did give students the opportunity to think for themselves. However, the court felt this was at the heart of the mission of public schools in this nation.

As a side comment, the court dealt with the quality of the U.S. history books. Both sides agreed, and the court agreed, that the books contained very little about the role of religion in U.S. history. The court indicated its task was not to judge the quality of the books, but to determine their legality. The books were returned to the classroom.

Another case further explained what government can do relative to course content. In this instance, Kenneth Roberts, a fifth grade teacher, gave his students 15 minutes a day for silent reading.[23] During this period, he sat at his desk and usually read from a Bible that he kept on his desk. Roberts claimed a violation of his rights to free exercise of religion, freedom of speech, and academic freedom after the principal ordered that he refrain from reading the Bible in his classroom. The school board claimed that allowing Roberts's behavior would violate the establishment clause. The court noted its need to balance Roberts's rights against students' rights to be free of religious influence or indoctrination in the classroom. Further, the court noted the great influence teachers have as role models, especially for children of this age. The principal's mandate was upheld.

Required Materials

The *Smith* case, discussed above, is applicable in this section. The course content essentially was dictated by the textbook content. As noted, the court upheld the authority of the board of education to select books for its classrooms despite the establishment clause claim of some unhappy parents.

At about the same time as *Smith*, the *Mozert* case arose in Hawkins County, Tennessee. [24] Several parents found the required basic reading series objectionable to their religious beliefs. They raised a challenge based on the free exercise clause of the First Amendment. In lieu of removing the books for all of the students, they wanted to have their children excused during the reading period so that they would not be exposed to ideas found in the books.

The court found no such violation of the First Amendment because there was no evidence that the students were required to say or do anything forbidden by their religion. Given the views of the plaintiffs, it would be virtually impossible to provide any books that would satisfy their objections because only their view of the world was the correct view. In effect, the school board would have to develop a curriculum that would foster only the religious views of the plaintiffs. This would violate the establishment clause. One of the tests of public schools is to teach tolerance of divergent views. One means of teaching such "civic tolerance" is based on presenting those views as a matter of information. The plaintiffs' claims were rejected.

Both the *Smith* and *Mozert* decisions support the authority of school boards to make curricular decisions relating to the use of books. What happens when the board chooses not to include a book? The *Virgil* case offers some insight. [25] A Florida school board decided to eliminate a textbook for a high school humanities course because of the inclusion of sexual content and vulgar language. Several parents filed suit claiming violation of their children's First Amendment right to receive information. A panel of judges of the Court of Appeals for the Eleventh Circuit upheld the decision of the school board, as it had done previously in *Smith*. Considering the "potentially sensitive topics," the court found the removal decision was "reasonably related to a legitimate pedagogical concern." This was a curriculum issue even though it was an elective course and the readings in the textbook involved were optional and not required. In addition, the court noted that the disputed readings had not been banned from the school completely, and no student or teacher was prohibited from assigning, reading, or discussing the materials or their themes.

A recent California case led to an opposite conclusion. [26] The school board voted to remove two books from the approved list of textbooks for an advanced twelfth grade English class. The trial judge had granted the school officials' motion to dismiss the case. Consequently, no evidence of board members' reasons for removal of these books was ever offered. In reversing the trial judge, the court remanded the case so that the teacher and other plaintiffs could have their opportunity to challenge the board members' reasons. However, the opinion seems to hold the defendants to a "tougher" standard to justify their action than required by the court in *Virgil*.

The previously mentioned case involving Kenneth Roberts raises two additional problems. He was ordered to remove two religiously oriented books from his classroom library. In addition, a Bible was ordered removed from the school library. The court dealt quickly with the religious books in the classroom library. It found the *The Bible in Pictures* and *The Story of Jesus* possessed no secular qualities. They were purely religious books and this distinction resulted in the court's approval of the principal's order to remove the books. The danger of indoctrinating students, according to the court, was too great. No claim to academic freedom could succeed because the two books were not related to any aspect of the approved curriculum for the fifth grade and Roberts offered no testimony about how he had used the books for the study of any facet of the curriculum.

Removing the Bible from the library presented a more difficult problem for the court. As the court ordered the Bible to be returned to the library, it noted:

> The school library is a mirror of the human race, repository of the works of scientists, leaders, and philosophers. It is the locus where the past meets tomorrow, embellished by the present....The Bible is regarded by many to be a major work of literature, history, ethics, theology, and philosophy. It has a legitimate, if not necessary, place in the American public school library.

Inclusion of religiously oriented books, including the Bible, reflects no preference for anything religious, according to the court.

While the *Roberts* case touched partially on the question of removal of a library book, the *Pico* case was entirely devoted to that question.[27] Nine books were ordered removed from elementary and secondary school libraries in the school system and their use in the curriculum was forbidden. Teachers were not forbidden from discussing the books or the ideas in the books. A student challenged this action by the school board as a violation of his First Amendment right to receive information. No trial was held as the district court granted the system's motion for summary judgment. No evidence was presented to identify board members' basis for the decision. In a decision that commanded no opinion for a majority of justices, the Court ordered the case be remanded for trial. Specifically, the plurality opinion held that school board members could not remove books in order to "prescribe what shall be orthodox in politics, nationalism, religion, or other matters of opinion." The board could make such

42

decisions based upon "educational suitability" of the books. A practical problem for the school board was the lack of any established, regular process for reviewing controversial materials.

Speakers / Assemblies / Plays

A high school student delivered a nominating speech for one of his friends.[28] He made the speech before approximately 600 students in grades 9 through 12 at a school-sponsored assembly. The principal found the speech to be completely inappropriate and suspended Matthew Fraser for three days and removed his name from the list of candidates for speaker at commencement exercises. Fraser claimed a violation of his right to freedom of speech.

Here is the speech that Fraser gave:

> I know a man who is firm—he's firm in his pants, he's firm in his shirt, his character is firm—but most of all, his belief in you, the students of Bethel, is firm.
> Jeff Kuhlman is a man who makes his point and pounds it in. If necessary, he'll take an issue and nail it to the wall. He doesn't attack things in spurts—he drives hard, pushing and pushing until finally—he succeeds.
> Jeff is a man who will go to the very end—even the climax, for each and every one of you.
> So vote for Jeff for A.S.B. vice president—he'll never come between you and the best our high school can be.

In upholding the decision of school officials, the Supreme Court found that the speech was indecent, obscene, and lewd. Such a speech would not be allowed in adult public circumstances. Coupling the location with the age of many of the students in the audience, the Court found Fraser's speech not to be protected by the First Amendment. In fact, the Court found that school officials had a responsibility, not just a right, to prohibit such public speaking in the school setting. The Court said: "The determination of what matter of speech in the classroom or in a school assembly is inappropriate properly rests with the school board."

It was not surprising two years later, when the Supreme Court faced a student's challenge to the principal's decision to censor two articles from a high school newspaper, that the students would lose.[29] The articles in question involved students' experiences with pregnancy and the impact of divorce on students at the school. The student claimed a right to free speech, while the principal claimed that as a curricular activity, he acted as a publisher would act. The Court held that school officials could exercise control over the style and content of speech in a school-sponsored activity "so long as their actions are reasonably related to legitimate pedagogical concerns."

Legitimate pedagogical concerns include the desire "to assure that participants learn whatever lessons the activity is designed to teach, that readers or listeners are not exposed to material that may be inappropriate to their level of maturity, and that the views of the individual speaker are not erroneously attributed to the school." Such standards give school officials massive discretion over the exercise of one's claimed constitutional rights at school.

How far does this massive discretion extend? In *Hazelwood*, the Court extended this authority to "school-sponsored publications, theatrical productions, and other expressive activities that students, parents and members of the public might reasonably perceive to bear the imprimatur of the school." If it is a "part of the school curriculum, supervised by faculty members, and designed to impart particular knowledge or skills to student participants and audiences," the school officials have vast authority.

Such a ruling was presaged by a decision of the Court of Appeals for the Third Circuit in 1981.[30] Several students unsuccessfully challenged the decision of the superintendent to cancel the proposed production of a musical that he felt would be inappropriate for school sponsorship. Finding the sexual theme of the play to be inappropriate and recognizing the decision as a typical administrative decision about curriculum and resources, the superintendent's decision stood.

Hazelwood in the Classroom

A mid-1989 case clearly catches the spirit of the current climate toward academic freedom. In *Krizek v. Board of Education*, an untenured English teacher claimed a violation of her academic freedom when she was not rehired for the next school year.[31]

Four months after Georgine Krizek showed an R-rated film (*About Last Night*) to her junior English class, a parent complained to a school administrator. The film concerned an unmarried couple's psychological and physical relationship. According to the court, there was "a great deal of vulgarity and sexually explicit scenes." No rule prohibited showing movies rated R or worse.

The judge made several salient points. First, academic freedom exists for the benefit of the student and society, not the teacher. Second, cases where a curriculum content rule exists must be treated in a legally different way than cases where no rule exists (as here). Third, the principles of *Hazelwood* (rather than principles from *Cooper, Mailloux, Keefe, Dean,* and *Parducci*) should apply to challenges against rules about curriculum content (as well as about newspapers, plays, etc.). Fourth, the principles of *Hazelwood* do apply to challenges where no rule exists, given the facts of this particular case.

Then the judge applied *Hazelwood* to Krizek's claim. He began by noting that administrators could have had "legitimate pedagogical concerns" justifying a specific rule against showing such films. And having such a rule (a "prior restraint") "is actually more permissible than after the fact punishment, unlike other areas of First Amendment law."

Even in the absence of a rule, school officials, with the recognized deference paid to their authority over curriculum, could reasonably find that showing this film offended "legitimate pedagogical concerns." However, was the sanction of nonrenewal too severe for the indiscretion? The judge found the vulgarity and sexual explicitness to be extensive and obvious. He found the length of the film and the planning of the showing indicated that this was "more than an inadvertent mistake or a mere slip of the tongue." The teacher's motion for an injunction to reverse the nonrenewal was unsuccessful.

CONCLUDING REMARKS

While several of the older cases seem to recognize a measure of academic freedom for the K–12 public school teacher,[32] more recent decisions have made clear that school boards enjoy broad authority to determine the curriculum, including which books are to be used. So long as school officials can articulate a legitimate pedagogical reason for their decision, it is likely that the courts will sustain the exercise of this broad authority.

To avoid the risk of losing their job, teachers should use common sense and avoid exposing their students to nonapproved materials such as R-rated movies that contain profanity and nudity and that are not appropriate for the age and maturity of K–12 students. Teachers also should obey any direct administrative order not to use certain materials, but should challenge such orders through appropriate grievance procedures or other administrative channels.

While an increasingly conservative judiciary is now unreceptive to claims of academic freedom, there are alternative means of protecting the teachers' freedom to teach. First, every school district should adopt a comprehensive procedure for processing parental complaints about "inappropriate" material in the classroom. Such procedures should provide for review of challenged books by a teacher-dominated committee that has the final say regarding the educational suitability of curriculum materials, library books, and outside reading lists. Second, local teacher associations should negotiate collective bargaining agreements that specifically recognize the academic freedom of classroom teachers and that give teachers the dominant say in determining curriculum content. Third, the state association should work for the passage of state laws that protect academic freedom and recognize the indispensable role of teachers in formulating local educational programs and policy.

Does this mean that the fight should not be carried on in the courts? Of course not. Judicial decrees are still the greatest long-term protection for academic freedom. Their struggle for academic freedom must never be abandoned if teachers want to fulfill their mission.

> To regard teachers—in our entire educational system, from the primary grades through the university—as the priests or our democracy is therefore not to indulge in hyperbole. It is the special task of teachers to foster those habits of open-mindedness and critical inquiry which alone make for responsible citizens, who, in turn, make possible an enlightened and effective public opinion. Teachers must fulfill their function by precept and practice, by the very atmosphere which they generate; they must be exemplars of open-mindedness and free inquiry. They cannot carry out their noble task if the conditions for the practice of a responsible and critical mind are denied to them.[33]

NOTES

1. *Sweezy v. New Hampshire*, 354 U.S. 234, 250 (1957).
2. *Keyishian v. Board of Regents*, U.S. 589, 603 (1967).
3. *Shelton v. Tucker* 364 U.S. 479, 487 (1960).
4. *Ahern v. Board of Education*, 456 F.2d 399 (8th Cir. 1972).
5. *Adams v. Campbell County S. D.*, 511 F.2d 1242 (10th Cir. 1975).
6. *Millikan v. Board of Directors*, 611 P.2d 414 (Wash. App. 1980); see *Clark v. Holmes*, 474 F.2d 928 (7th Cir. 1972), cert. denied 411 U.S. 972 (1973).
7. *Keefe v. Geanakos*, 418 F.2d 359 (1st Cir. 1969); see *Mailloux v. Kiley*, 448 F.2d 1242 (1st Cir. 1971). *Contra Harris v. Mechanicsville Central S.D.*, 408 N.Y.S.2d 384 (1978).
8. *Parducci v. Rutland*, 316 F.Supp. 352 (M.D. Ala. 1970).
9. *Brubaker v. Board of Education*, 502 F.2d 973 (7th Cir. 1974).
10. *Fisher v. Fairbanks North Star Borough S.D.*, 704 P.2d 213 (Alaska 1985).
11. *Cary v. Board of Education*, 598 F.2d 535 (10th Cir. 1979). See also *Loewen v. Turnipseed*, 488 F. Supp. 1138 (N.D. Miss. 1980).
12. *Kingsville Independent S.D. v. Cooper*, 611 F.2d 1109 (5th Cir. 1980).
13. *Sterzing v. Fort Bend Independent S.D.*, 496 F.2d 92 (5th Cir. 1974).
14. *Dean v. Timpson Independent S.D.*, 486 F. Supp. 302 (E.D. Tex. 1979); see *Oakland Unified S.D. v. Olicker*, 25 C.A. 3d 1098 (Cal. App. 1972); and *Beebee v. Haslett Public Schools*, 239 N.W.2d 724 (Mich. App. 1976).
15. *Dale v. Board of Education*, 316 N.W.2d 108 (S.D. 1982).
16. *Burns v. Rovaldi*, 477 S. Supp. 270 (D. Conn. 1979). See also *LaRocca v. Board of Education*, 406 N.Y.S.2d 348 (App. Div. 1978).
17. *Jergeson v. Board of Trustees*, 476 P.2d 481 (Wyo. 1970).

18. *Celestine v. Lafayette Parish School Board*, 284 S.2d 650 (La. App. 1973); and *Frison v. Franklin County Board of Education*, 596 F.2d 1192 (4th Cir. 1979).

19. *Wilson v. Chancellor*, 418 F. Supp. 1358 (D. Ore. 1976).

20. *Solmitz v. Maine School Administrative District No. 59*, 495 A.2d 812 (Me. 1985).

21. *Edwards v. Board of School Commissioners*, 482 U.S. 578 (1987).

22. *Smith v. Board of School Commissioners*, 827 F.2d 684 (11th Cir. 1987).

23. *Roberts v. Madigan*, 702 F. Supp. 1505 (D. Colo. 1989). This case has been appealed.

24. *Mozert v. Hawkins County Board of Education*, 827 F.2d 1058 (6th Cir. 1987).

25. *Virgil v. School Board*, 826 F.2d 1517 (11th Cir. 1989); see also *Bicknell v. Vergennes Union High School Board of Directors*, 638 F.2d 438 (2d Cir. 1980).

26. *McCarthy v. Fletcher*, 254 Cal. Rptr. 714 (Cal. App. 1989).

27. *Board of Education v. Pico*, 457 U.S. 853 (1982).

28. *Bethel S.D. v. Fraser*, 478 U.S. 675 (1986).

29. *Hazelwood S.D. v. Kuhlmeier*, 108 Sup. Ct. 515 (1987).

30. *Seyfried v. Walton*, 668 F.2d 214 (3d Cir. 1981).

31. 713 F. Supp. 1131 (N.D. 111 1989). For a case with similar facts and a similar result, see *Fowler v. Board of Education*, 819 F.2d 657 (6th Cir. 1987).

32. For a comprehensive legal analysis, see Goldstein, *The Asserted Constitutional Right of Public School Teachers to Determine What They Teach*, 124 U. Pa. L. Rev. 1293 (1976); Kemmer & Hirsh, *The Developing Law Involving the Teacher's Right To Teach*, 84 W. Va. L. Rev. 31 (1981); and Small, *A Legal Framework for Academic Freedom in Public Secondary Schools*, 12 J. of L. & Ed. 529 (1983).

33. *Wieman v. Updegraff*, 344 U.S. 183, 196 (1952).

4. ACADEMIC FREEDOM AND COMMUNITY INVOLVEMENT: MAINTAINING THE BALANCE

by Arnold F. Fege, Director, National PTA
Office of Governmental Relations

A profound clash of values is increasingly being played out in our public schools. The broader conflict revolves around a very wide range of beliefs regarding religion, creationism, sex education, values education, and secular humanism. The freedom to read or teach any publication is being threatened by well-organized community groups, state legislatures, and the courts. The more specific battle focuses on the role of the public school in either capitulating to censorship attempts, or assuring a balanced, open, and robust curriculum providing for a free exchange of ideas.

Academic freedom is under attack. It is almost impossible to convey the fervor of emotions, behaviors, and contentions ignited by censorship battles at the school and community levels. Local control of education, a privilege with substantive political resonance, is easily exploited by those who would suppress materials or ideas that they find objectionable. During the past decade, America's censors took aim at the public school curriculum and targeted an array of courses, textbooks, teaching methods, and materials, as well as a wide assortment of books, plays, and audiovisual materials.

These actions reflect not only the growing vocalism of the Far Right and fundamentalists, but also a backlash against the development of new curriculum materials and the worries of some that our traditional democratic beliefs and values that define us as a people are not holding up too well in today's world.

For instance, in Hawkins County, Tennessee, parents raised objections to the Holt, Rinehart and Winston reading series in a 1986 Supreme Court case, *Mozert v. Hawkins County*.[1] The parents said they objected to students using their imaginations "beyond the limitation of scriptural authority." They raised 47 objections to stories that introduced students to beliefs and practices of religious groups and world religions other than those shared by the plaintiffs; they raised 24 objections to the teaching of evolution, they objected to stories introducing students to global problems and stressing the need for international cooperation; and they objected to portraying modern roles of men and women. One of the de-

48

fendants testified that "the Lord has set down Biblical government, roles for men and women." Although the Supreme Court subsequently denied the parents' contention that they could "opt out" of the reading program, the case epitomizes a movement led by such organizations as Citizens for Excellence in Education, the Moral Majority, the Eagle Forum, Mel and Norma Gabler's Education Research Analysts, and the Free Congress Research and Education Foundation—all of whom object to materials and curriculum contrary to Christian doctrines, discussion of topics such as birth control and homosexuality, presentations of a variety of concepts that are controversial such as death and dying, and teaching of "secular humanism."

Perhaps encouraged by the Reagan administration's push for officially sanctioned school prayer, tuition tax credits, and the new political power of fundamentalist conservatives, the censors are moving against public schools when they teach anything that conflicts with their views. This climate raises questions about the definition of academic freedom in the context of public education, parental involvement, and a pluralistic society.

Certainly, social and demographic changes have contributed to censorship tensions. Under the rhetoric of school improvement and educational reform, we are living through an unprecedented reactionary period. All periods of history seem to be "of transition," and the sources and impact of change are seldom evident except in retrospect. Even the most parent-oriented student of American social forces cannot fail to notice changes today that are remarkably deep and quick.

Indeed, the changing picture recalls Henry Adams's impressions at the dawn of the 20th century—"a far faster universe, where all the old roads ran about in every direction, overrunning, dividing, subdividing, stopping abruptly, vanishing slowly, with side paths that led nowhere and consequences that could not be proved." For educators, this past decade has been a time of change and community upheaval. Public schools are "public" not only because they are free, but because they are charged with crating citizens. Shaping character, transmitting common civic values, and nourishing critical thinking to future generations is as vital a task as teaching reading.

We are subsequently weaving our way through forceful constitutional, legal, social, and moral questions. Those questions are the most fundamental that can be addressed by parents and by this nation as we go about the business of redefining what is common among us—the business of redefining the common school. Those questions are the balance-wheel questions of academic freedom posed by the current wave of attacks on public school curriculum, materials, and books. They include such questions as the following:

49

1. How shall we be able to accommodate the compelling interests of the state in our children's education and the individual interest of the parent?

The state has reserved for itself broad discretionary powers over elementary and secondary education. Some of these powers such as regulations pertaining to compulsory attendance, finance equity, textbook selection, course requirements, safety codes, health and environmental guidelines, and bonding procedures, the state has deemed so important as to be "compelling" and in the best interest of *all* of the children. There are times when these interests are fundamentally incompatible with the special interests of parents, especially when children are required to read books that parents believe are "profane" or "damaging" to their children or when schools require all children to take particular courses such as sex education that parents find objectionable.

2. How do we frame educational policies so that meaningful parental involvement in education for all is not exploited by the few parents for special interest ends?

Community support of the public school program and its curriculum is one essential component in community acceptance and ownership. At issue is how to develop policies that meet the democratic ends of a balanced program open to a variety of diverse ideas without also opening up the process to a well-monied, well-organized community group powerful enough to control the decision-making process toward their own private interests. Examples of such groups could be a political party, the Chamber of Commerce, a religious organization, or a parent organization. Building a system of checks and balances is essential in preventing abuses.

3. How can academic freedom be maintained while still addressing unique parental and community needs?

In the process of designing programs that are "community-sensitive," the role of teachers in exercising their rights of academic freedom in either accepting or countermanding community preferences should be defined. The freedom that teachers have in selecting the curriculum, outside readings, library books and/or curriculum strategies often differs from state to state and district to district. With an increase in parental involvement and more interest by the community in influencing education, does this mean the decision-making freedoms that teachers have exercised over the years will diminish? While the teacher's right to teach

50

and select classroom material has been generally accepted, few would deny this freedom has had its limits, and is threatened with each censorship attempt.

4. How do we define intellectual freedom while simultaneously guaranteeing the individual complainants' right to be heard?

Would-be censors are not unbalanced, radical, or otherwise fiendish troublemakers. They are usually people who have a concern that school materials or programs will actually corrupt their children. The problem is that they believe the materials will corrupt other students as well, and they seek to deny the entire school community the use of certain books, materials or programs. Policies should be developed to hear the sincere complaints of parents, but to ensure that the right for all children to learn and to express ideas without fear of censorship is protected. Complaints of individual parents should be reconciled with clearly articulated and professionally developed objectives protecting intellectual freedom. While parents have the right to complain, they do not have the right to limit educational opportunities for the entire community.

5. How does a school district encourage academic freedom while a group of parents are badgering the school board and threatening to restrict educational opportunities?

Just the mere threat of a censorship campaign may have a chilling effect on the decisions made by boards of education. Boards who wish to avoid conflict may subtly and informally restrict academic freedom by approving materials that are noncontroversial, or may bypass existing material selection and complaint policies in an effort to placate a vocal minority of parents who wish to ban certain material from the library and classroom. A school board's commitment to free expression may give way to even the threat of a noisy and troublesome censoring group. After all, boards of education are primarily political creatures that are prone to political pressures. Indeed, censoring groups have been known to run their own candidates for the board of education with the single interest of imposing their viewpoint on the curriculum.

6. How can a public school deal with "moral convictions" that make for good education without, by that very fact, offending the consciences of some parents compelled by law to enroll their children?

A legitimate function of the public schools is to teach values. Tension arises, however, when values education becomes confused with morality.

51

Thomas Lickona, a developmental psychologist at the State University of New York, makes a distinction between "public morality" and "private morality." He defines private morality as those values dealing with religious beliefs, while defining public morality as universal values to which we are all obligated, like it or not. Many schools choose to stay away from private morality, which they believe is better left to the home and church to teach. Some parents disagree and contend that religious beliefs should be part of the school curriculum. An objective of the Citizens for Excellence in Education (CEE), an arm of the National Association of Christian Educators (NACE), is "to bring public education back under the control of Christians and to change the atheist-dominated idealogy of secular humanism in our schools, texts, curriculum and teachers unions." On the other hand, schools that do decide to take the more controversial plunge into teaching "about" religion, emphasizing a balanced, neutral viewpoint without denominational preference, risk taking a shot from parents who believe no mention of religion should be allowed, or from parents who do not want their children exposed to any religion except theirs. The current push for teaching about values, while a legitimate educational function, is loaded with the potential from community groups to exploit the community debate by including their own brand of religion.

These questions go to the heart of the issue, the purposes, the raison d'être of public schools. These are two competing views of public education. One supports the premise that schools should expand the knowledge base of students, exposing them to a variety of ideas so that they can function more effectively in a pluralistic and changing society. Some parents, however, seek a narrower, more basic curriculum that limits the exposure their children would have to certain ideas, books, and intstructional materials. From their point of view, the public schools are competing with their family values and beliefs. If the centrifugal force of this polarization is to be kept in check, school districts must attend to the following policy quesitons: Who determines what is to be taught in the public schools, and how? Who takes charge of the necessary balancing between education and socialization, between the communication of diverse ideas, and the inculcation of common values?

If the school's role is seen primarily as one of indoctrination and inculcation of community values, school boards may have almost unlimited discretion in the selection and removal of materials that are part of the schools' curriculum. However, if the view is that the school is a marketplace of ideas where students may have access to a variety of viewpoints, the limits imposed upon the school board are expanded considerably. At different times, both views have been upheld by the courts at all levels around the country.

To compound the issue, more and more legislation at the federal and state levels include explicit provisions that parents and community be involved in part of all aspects of the program as a condition for the school district to receive funding. For instance, in the newly reauthorized federal Chapter 1 aid for disadvantaged children program, P.L. 100–297, the law now requires that parents be involved in the design, implementation, and evaluation of the program. A newly passed AIDS education program, P.L. 100–607, circumscribes the focus of the curriculum to the teaching of factual and accurate information, with an emphasis on safe sex and the requirement that parents be involved at both the state and local levels in any AIDS curriculum that may be developed, recommended, or mandated. The same provisions are likely to be written into other pending legislation such as vocational education, bilingual education, school-based health clinics, child care, Chapter 2 Block Grants, and a host of other measures passed by state legislatures. Many parent and child advocacy organizations support these provisions, but prefer to leave the specifics of such involvement to the discretion of state departments of education and local school districts. The purpose of such requirements is to assure a broad base of community participation, which, hopefully, will mitigate attempts at censorship, while responding to the needs of the community.

Other statutes, however, were passed that exploited the parental involvement movement. In 1984, "secular humanism," the Far Right's codeword for whatever it has determined as objectionable, found its way into federal law, at least for two years. Removed through the amendment process in 1986, a provision pushed by the Far Right would have prohibited the use of magnet school monies to teach "secular humanism." Also, in 1984, the scope of the original "Pupil Rights Protection Act," the so-called Hatch Amendment, was expanded by the regulations issued by the U.S. Department of Education. The new regulation[2] goes beyond the intent of the original legislation, which now requires that parental consent be obtained for psychiatric and psychological tests before they are administered to children. The regulations are so broad and so vague that they are being used as a basis for assaults at the local level on classroom discussion, curriculum, and school activities, which could be construed as comprising a "psychological or psychiatric test." Not content with federal law, attempts were made to pass "Baby Hatch Amendments" in at least eight states.

In yet another wrinkle regarding the balance between academic freedom and community involvement, the New York State School Boards Associaton has sued the State Commissioner of Education for passing certain regulations that they say require the school boards to violate the establishment clause of the First Amendment of the United States Constitution. The object of the lawsuit is Commissioner's regulations section 135.3 (b) (2) and (c) (2), which mandates that school boards appoint an AIDS advisory council including church representation. This council is responsible for making recommendations to the school board concerning AIDS instruction in the public school.

The New York School Boards Association contends that these regulations place school districts in the precarious position of determining which religious organizations and which viewpoints, if any, should be incorporated into a district's AIDS curriculum. They argue that a public school board must never be placed in the position of choosing from within the religious community.

It is clear at the elementary and secondary levels that the same academic freedoms guaranteed to university professors are not as absolutely assured to school teachers. Authority of school boards, preemptions through legislation, court and case law, and practice have all worked to narrow the parameters of academic freedom accorded to teachers.

Owing to the vast realm of concerns, possibilities, and options that the academic freedom area presents, every school district must work through policies to advance democratic ends. Those ends should emphasize materials and curricula that promote diversity, pluralism, and tolerance in a democratic society, and opposition to those who would restrict, rather than expand the intellectual realm for students.

Cries that society is disintegrating are hardly unprecedented. They have been repeated generation after generation, even when prayers were said daily and church attendance was higher. Concern that an America in which religion is not the most powerful social force is doomed has been a commonplace of conservative religious thought, particularly within the American Protestant tradition, for a century. The emphasis on prayer, a personal acknowledgement of God's sovereignty, a belief that creation is the only possible belief to explore the world's beginnings, are all respectable religious positions. They are not, however, the only possible positions, and in any event, are not plausible premises for narrowing the curriculum or purging other ideas.

Despite their diversity of strategies and tactics, all interested in protecting the freedom to learn—whether involved in censorship controversy or trying to prevent one—come to two univesal conclusions:

1. Protecting the freedom to learn is much easier if a school system had adopted formal selection policies to set academic standards and spell out goals, and reconsideration procedures to resolve disputes in an orderly democratic manner;
2. It is essential to organize the broadest possible base of support for academic freedom and against censorship.

More important are the central questions raised by Hatch and other related laws: how can parents be involved in the review and selection of materials in a meaninful, legitimate way? In other words, how can parents be involved in a way that strengthens the instructional program for *all* children rather than destroy it through banning attempts. Parents should not control, but should have the right to be involved.

Every school system should have a comprehensive written policy in the selection of all instructional and library materials. A selection policy will help define the goals of the school and provide a format for resolution, before the heat of a challenge to materials occurs. In a crisis, when there are complaints about social studies texts, human development materials, or library books, the inclusion of a particular material can be justified and explained in accordance with preestablished school principles. A school district selection policy should include—

1. Specific goals of the instructional program,
2. The goals and objectives of the library and media center,
3. A description of all steps in the selection process from the initial screening to final selection and the particular committee responsible for each step,
4. Procedure for periodic reviews of existing materials to allow for reassessment when the curriculum changes,
5. A definition of who has final authority for instructional materials selection,
6. Established procedures for handling complaints and to select materials,
7. The inclusion of parents and community on a selection review committee.

These policies should be formulated with input from a wide variety of sources, but the ultimate responsibility for material selection lies with the school board and professional staff. They also, however, do not have the right to impose their personal political, religious, social, or aesthetic beliefs or biases on students. They also must abide by the objective criteria as contained in the policies. Remember, policy will not necessarily reduce the number of complaints, but it can be used as a tool to—

1. Educate the community,
2. Provide some ownership for parents in the selection process,
3. Allow for a more rational response to community grievances, and
4. Establish a framework in which parents can become involved.

Many school districts around the country have already developed fair and democratic review procedures offering parents a meaningful role in the selection of materials. In Prince George's County, Maryland, for instance, more than 40 review committees examine reading material before recommending for approval by the Board of Education. Each four-member review committee includes a lay person, usually a parent or PTA person, as a voting member. Before any textbook can be approved, all members of a committee must agree that it is appropriate. The decision is reached through a detailed examination, which includes a study of such items as absence of racial or sex stereotyping, accuracy of information, and readability.

This is in contrast to a Panama City, Florida School Board adopted policy that requires all instructional materials to be approved by the superintendent prior to their use in the classrooms. The arbitrariness of the school policy allowed the superintendent to ban one book, *I Am the Cheese*, even though 88 of 92 parents signed slips permitting the use of the book, which received a national award from the National Council of Teachers of English for its innovative curriculum. Subsequently, the superintendent removed 64 books from the classroom, many of which were classics including Chaucer's *Canterbury Tales*, Shakespeare's *King Lear*, and *Wuthering Heights*.

In Prince George's County, during the past seven years, no formal textbook complaints have been issued, and only seven complaints about library books have been received. In one complaint, a parent objected to the "inappropriate language" in a library book called *The Thief*, by Thomas Rockwell. That parent was invited to describe her concerns to a committee of nine people, which in this case agreed with her. The book was removed from a list of approved materials.

In Panama City, on the other hand, the superintendent's actions stirred an anticensorship group and an emotionally charged atmosphere enveloped the community as those opposed to the book banning took their case to the media, to school board meetings, and to the courts. Ultimately, the school board was forced to change its selection policy, but not before an outbreak of violence against several teachers and a local television reporter ensued.

Different points of view always will exist about instructional material. The essential point, however, is that well-defined, uniformly administered, fair and open procedures should be established. Such procedures help avoid extreme positions and crises such as that in Panama City.

Parents and communities concerned about the dangerous attacks on the free exchange of ideas must be prepared to act on their convictions. While it is not the most comfortable endeavor, going around mopping up after acts of censorship is a job somebody has to do. Censors take advantage of their audience's ignorance in a number of ways. First, through the double speak of censorship theology, which often confuses rational debate, parental involvement has come to mean control; equal time, to mean inclusion of religious instruction in the curriculum; secular humanism, to mean anything except the views of the censor; back to basics, to mean going back to Christian values and imposing them on everyone else; sex respect, to mean opposition to teaching a more well-balanced and comprehensive sex education curriculum; values education, to mean the teaching of Judeo-Christian religion to the exclusion of other religions.

Second, censors project a view that they have a majority of the community sentiment. Through skillful manipulation of petition drives, public rallies, and media attention, would-be censors may appear to command broad support even if their forces are quite small. A key to dealing with any censorship campaign is to mobilize support of the silent majority and give it voice and power. The goal is to encourage fruitful discussion and debate of issues. If indeed, the campaign for censorship does include a majority of the community, the counter-campaign will be especially difficult. The broader the base of the coalition to include organizations such as the PTA, child-related associations, civil rights, and religious groups, the more credibility is increased.

Third, censorship issues are frequently presented as a test of religious faith. While the religious faith of the censors should not be doubted or questioned, their error is not one of religion, but of policy. God has taken no position on the U.S. Department of Education, school-linked health clinics, Houghton Mifflin reading texts, MACOS, or psychological tests. Religious values cannot be excluded from every public issue—but not every public issue involves religious values. Each school district has an obligation to teach those values that are common—honesty, citizenship, patriotism, cooperation, tolerance, democracy, truthfulness. The issue is not between sectarianism and nonsectarianism. The Constitution draws that line for us.

Fourth, while current censorship attempts are from the Far Right, the history of censorship has included attacks from the left as well. Minorities who object to the treatment of Afro-Americans in *Huckleberry Finn*, or feminists who object to sexual portrayals of women in certain magazines, or ethnics who challenge the historical veracity or interpretation of particular events in a social studies text have all been numbered among the would-be censors of the past. While all censorship attempts should be countered, it is helpful to listen to the objections of the complainants, and know the reasons for their concerns. Overacting or generalizing about the complainants or their challenge may unnecessarily prejudice your ability to work out a satisfactory resolution. Educators need to avoid engaging in "we" and "they," "hero" or "villain" dichotomies. A firm stance against censorship, while respecting opinions of the complainant may keep an easily resolvable issue from escalating.

Should you as a teacher in a school district be confronted with a major censorship controversy, I recommend the following ideas that would be of help to you in dealing with the issue:

1. As a teacher, you need to make sure that noncensorship provisions are included in school policies and that you take an active role in the development of such policy.
2. As a teacher, you play a major role in educating the community about selection policies, the materials used in the curriculum, and the importance of an educational program that presents a factual, diverse, accurate, and wide-ranging view of the world.
3. Do not shy away from controversial subjects and topics that meet the criteria of your policy. Remember, when censorship attempts do succeed, that usually leads to other attempts at censorship. When a balanced curriculum succeeds, that usually means an exciting, relevant instructional program and an informed community.
4. When a complaint is received, your initial response as a teacher is to listen to it. Find out what concerns motivate this complaint and try to understand the nature of the material in question and educational practice. Most important, at the early stages, it is important to have a rational justification for the material. Do not take a complaint as a personal attack! This is not a decision-making time.
5. Treat all complaints with respect and do not jump to conclusions. Those who complain about educational materials vary widely in their life experience, educational level, and their understanding of academic freedom. Virtually all hold sincere and deeply rooted convictions. Maintain your cool and dignity at all times. No material, however, should be removed without the formal review.
6. As a teacher, an attack on your choice of content or teaching strategies requires that you identify a support group that will stand by you throughout the episode. Friends, families, colleagues, your teachers organizations are sorely needed at such times. You will be stronger as a result of such support and weaker if you go through it alone.

Many local censorship incidents still consist of one parent complaining about one book. Please note that in most cases parents and community will support a broadly based education program. But more frequently, complaints involve community organizing attempts to establish or change local policy, to apply more pressure at the selection process stage as well as efforts to run single-interest candidates for school boards. Some local groups, with outside help and money, are introducing and lobbying for restrictive state legislation and, when all else fails, they are suing teachers, principals, and school districts, claiming their rights. If experience is our guide, it is precisely those school districts that are largely homogeneous and where the danger of oppression of religious minorities is greatest, that would permit censorship of new and different ideas. The ultimate victims are children.

If the battle becomes brutal, the next step is to form a community-wide coalition. The purpose is not to draw lines, but rather, to create a series of intelligent, well-calculated strategies based on the high ground: unhysterical, but firm; focused on issues and not on people and personalities; arguments based on facts, not emotions. Indeed, censorship campaigns are often effectively stopped by a forthright challenge to the would-be censors to put their demands on the line. If nothing else, such a challenge prevents the censors from continually shifting their rhetoric to confuse the issue. At stake is nothing more than the public school. Parents can and should be involved in the education of their children, whether selecting a school from a list of attractive magnet school offerings, supporting budget requests, assisting children with school assignments, or volunteering. Their involvement must not impose their own values by narrowing the content and the program.

"Stay away from the wrong books, Yakov, the impure." "There are no wrong books. What's wrong is the fear of them" (Bernard Malamud, from *The Fixer*).

NOTES

1. *Bob Mozert, et. al. v. Hawkins County Public Schools, et. al.* Petition for a Writ of Certiorari to the United States Court of Appeals for the Sixth Circuit, October Term, 1987.
2. *Federal Register 34 CFR Parts 75, 76, and 98.* September 6, 1984.

5. LESSONS LEARNED FROM THREE SCHOOLBOOK PROTESTS

by Edward B. Jenkinson, Professor of English Education,
Indiana University

Myths about schoolbook protests mask reality. Some teachers and administrators spread myths as if they were gospel, and their acceptance as truth sometimes makes it difficult for participants in censorship incidents to deal effectively with their plight. Here are some common myths:

Attempts to censor school materials occur mainly in the Bible Belt;

Irate citizens in small towns are more likely to attempt to rid the schools of so-called offensive books than people in cities;

Rural communities are more likely to experience censorship than cities and suburbs;

Appointed school boards censor more books than elected ones;

All parents want their children to be well-read and to think critically;

Parents do not want public schools to advance particular religious beliefs;

Textbooks adopted on a statewide basis are not likely to be attacked by anyone;

Literary classics are beyond reproach;

Rational argument will save any book, course, film, or teaching method.

Perhaps the most unrealistic belief is that censorship "can't happen here." Attempts to remove textbooks, library books, films, courses, and teaching methods can occur anywhere—in every state, in every size city and town, in schools at every socioeconomic level. And the "it can't happen here" syndrome leaves people ill-prepared to cope with even a mild protest.

The state of Indiana experiences no more schoolbook protests than any other state. In fact, for its size and population it probably ranks, proportionally, below most states in the East, West, and South. But three incidents in Indiana—all occurring in cities of under 20,000 population—are most instructive. Spread over a decade, they started near the top of the

60

state at Warsaw, moved down to Tell City on the Ohio River, and then shifted only a few miles north to Oakland City in Gibson County. Each incident had distinct characteristics, participants, tactics, and resolutions. But each made significant contributions to a pool of information that might help teachers learn how to prepare for, and cope with, a censorship incident.

On December 15, 1977, the Warsaw *Times-Union* first published a chilling news photo that has been reprinted in newspapers and magazines throughout the nation and has been flashed across television screens. The picture of a smiling group of senior citizens standing by a trash can filled with burning textbooks shocked newspaper readers in dozens of cities. To some, it signaled the grim fact that book burning can—and does—happen in America.

The consignment of 40 copies of Sidney Simon's *Values Clarification* to senior citizens for burning was only one in a series of school board actions that paralyzed the academic community in Warsaw. And, according to several teachers with whom I have talked, anxiety still walks school corridors and haunts classrooms.

The Warsaw *Times-Union* played a major role in the schoolbook war in this city of 10,000 that is surrounded by rich loam soil in northeastern Indiana. A community that labels itself conservative, it boasts of thriving small industries, very low unemployment, and a "strong religious feeling." Its citizens have their choice of 63 churches, and the community is proud of its church-affiliated college on Winona Lake.

The harmony of Warsaw was shattered by discordant notes in 1977 and 1978. Reporters descended on the town; camera crews of nationally prominent programs parked their trucks on the streets several times. Angry citizens, many of them protesting books they had not read in their entirety, wrote letters to the editor, and former friends stopped talking. Schoolbooks divided the town.

A brief description of the major actions in the schoolbook controversy follows.

1. Shortly after William Chapel joined the appointed board, he called for an evaluation of the Individually Guided Education Program (IGE) in one elementary school. The board contracted for an outside evaluation of the program during the last three days of school. People in Warsaw doubted that any program could be evaluated effectively during the last week of school. The supporters of IGE were outraged. So was Max E. Hobbs, the superintendent who had brought the IGE program to Warsaw; he resigned after seven years in the community. After the evaluation, the board met for 15 minutes in a closed session and dropped the program.[1]

2. At the next board meeting, Mr. Chapel asked for an evaluation of *Values Clarification* and the class in which it was used. According to the *Times-Union*, "It took only a few minutes of reading passages from the text for the school board's reaction to throw the book out and discontinue the English class that once used it." In his motion, one board member said that the book should be "thrown out, removed, banned, destroyed and forbidden to be used."

The teacher who used the book insisted that only 10 of the approximately 200 exercises were used in classes elected by students who have academic and social problems. The course and the text became part of the English program after the Indiana Department of Public Instruction conducted an in-service training program on values clarification two years before the course was eliminated.

The teacher who had used parts of the condemned textbook in her class left the community shortly after the board decided the fate of the course and the book. She told me that she could not accept the fact that a board would act so harshly and emotionally on a course and book about which board members had so little information. She said that no one wanted to hear her side of the story; she was so devastated by the experience that she "virtually became a vegetable" for more than a year.

3. Only 42 days after he was appointed superintendent, Dr. Charles Bragg announced major changes in the high school English curriculum. Without consulting Mrs. Arleen Miner, the English department chairperson, the board decided to replace three unspecified courses with two composition courses. Mrs. Miner resigned, noting that the board had been misinformed since five composition classes were already in the program.

Dr. Bragg called for the discontinuation of the following courses at the beginning of the second semester: Gothic Literature, Black Literature, Science Fiction, Good Guys, Folklore and Legends, Detective and Mystery Fiction, and Whatever Happened to Mankind. He also announced that the phase-elective English program would be eliminated at the end of the academic year.

4. Before the new superintendent arrived, Teresa Burnau ordered copies of the following books for a course entitled "Women in Literature": *The Stepford Wives, Go Ask Alice, The Bell Jar, Growing Up Female in America, The Feminine Plural: Stories by Women About Growing Up*, and *The New Women: A Motive Anthology of Women's Liberation*. Shortly after the books arrived in the fall, the principal gave them "a cursory examination." Mr. Smith told Ms. Burnau to return *Growing Up Female in America* to the publisher because it contained

pictures of nude women. She agreed to return the copies, noting the book was to be used as supplementary material in a course whose enrollment was entirely girls.

Later that same day, Mr. Smith told Ms. Burnau she could not use *The Stepford Wives* in the course. Six weeks into the course, he told her to stop teaching *Go Ask Alice* because it "was found to be objectionable by patrons of our school." When she told the principal that the girls in the class had nearly finished reading the book, he told her to let them finish reading it. Then in a supervisor's conference report, he commented: "You were advised to discontinue the use of any reading materials that contained these kinds of obscenities. A guideline to follow is not to use any reading materials in your classes that would cause you embarrassment if you were asked to read these materials to our governing body."

With less than six weeks remaining in "Women in Literature," the principal instructed Ms. Burnau not to use Sylvia Plath's *The Bell Jar* in her class. The teacher protested in writing, pointing out that it was too late for her to order another book. When she was told she would be dismissed for insubordination if she taught the book, she dropped it from the course.

It needs to be pointed out here that in his long tenure in Warsaw, the principal had never before ordered teachers to stop teaching books. Only after the new superintendent arrived and issued a directive about "objectionable" books did the principal begin interfering with classroom instruction.

On his staff appraisal report, Mr. Smith marked Ms. Burnau as satisfactory (the highest mark) on 14 of 18 items. He noted that she is "an excellent classroom teacher and is doing a fine job in teaching Composition I this second semester." He also noted that she had taught *Go Ask Alice*, a book considered to be objectionable, and that she displayed "resentment and a poor attitude" when she was told not to teach *The Bell Jar*.

Noting her inability "to handle professional direction in a positive manner," Dr. Bragg sent Ms. Burnau a letter at the end of April informing her that her contract would not be renewed.

5. On October 10, the minutes of the school board contained these two sentences attributed to Dr. Bragg: [He] states there are some books in question at this time. He states a directive was issued to principals in the third week of August asking them to respond to him about any books that were in poor taste, and that responses have been received. On October 18, Mr. Smith sent this directive to all teachers in the high school: "Any classroom materials that you have in your room that might be objectionable, please bring them to the office."

63

Mrs. Milner responded to the directive by showing Mr. Smith portions of a literature textbook she had used for at least three years in her senior English classes. She pointed to a few words, including *damn* and *hell*, and asked Mr. Smith if they were objectionable. The principal said they were, and tried to black them out but the ink bled through. He then told the chairperson to remove the pages from the book. She did so in her classroom by using scissors to cut four pages from each copy of the text. The students noted that she was visibly shaken and that she trembled as she collected the books and cut out the pages.

6. On January 4, 1978, the Warsaw Community Education Association (WCEA) filed a complaint with the Indiana Education Employment Relations Board. The complaint, which was considered the largest and most complex ever filed by teachers in Indiana, charged the school board with 11 infractions, including unilaterally—

a. changing the curriculum of one elementary school by removing IGE;

b. unilaterally and forcibly transferring four teachers from the elementary school where IGE was used;

c. banning an English textbook;

d. changing the high school English curriculum;

e. administering an arbitrary and capricious textbook censorship program.

7. On January 9, 1978, Mr. Chapel read this resolution, which the board passed unanimously: "Be it resolved that teachers, administrators and staff of this school shall be directed to teach students to avoid use of profanity and obscenities, and also books and materials that could be construed as objectionable in this community shall not be used."

8. In April, 11 teachers were asked to resign. Ms. Burnau and two others refused; they were dismissed. JoAnn DuPont, secretary of the WCEA, had taught in Warsaw for five years and had received positive performance appraisals. A teacher of business who set up her classes as if the students were working on the job, she was stunned when she received a letter from Dr. Bragg, stating that her contract would not be renewed. Dr. Bragg charged her with (a) drinking coffee in her room; (b) allowing students to drink pop and eat candy at their desks in the business practice room; (c) allegedly allowing her daughter to be in her room when the school bus dropped her off from the parochial school at 2:49 in the afternoon.

An outspoken parent-critic of the school board declared that the WCEA secretary was "an outstanding business teacher who was fired for being an outspoken teacher and an officer of the WCEA." Mrs. DuPont had written a letter to the editor of the *Times-Union*, protesting the school board's actions. That, apparently, was the unwritten cause of her dismissal.

The Indiana State Teachers Association filed complaints against the school board in behalf of the two fired teachers. ISTA claimed that their dismissal violated their First Amendment rights. Both settled out of court. Ms. Burnau moved to the East and, to my knowledge, never taught again. Mrs. DuPont is a professor in a college about 15 miles from Warsaw.

9. The editor of the high school newspaper wrote an editoral expressing her dismay at the dismissal and forced resignations of the teachers. Mr. Smith stopped publication of the newspaper until the editor called the Student Press Law Center in Washington, D.C., and threatened to appeal the principal's decision to the school board. The principal let the newspaper be published.

10. At the end of the school year, Mr. Smith was replaced by a new principal.

11. During the summer, the new principal called the editor and her parents into his office and asked the editor to resign. She refused. When he did not permit the newspaper to be published during the following year, the editor sued. Her case was dismissed in federal court without trial.

12. Shortly before the unfair labor practice hearing began in June, the *Times-Union* published editorials, news stories, and editorial cartoons that left no doubt in the readers' minds that the newspaper was opposed to the hearing, to the books, and to the teachers who had been dismissed. Two weeks before the hearing, Carl Davis, a school patron, read excepts of *Go Ask Alice* at a school board meeting, and the newspaper published the passages with a note on the front page urging reader caution.

During the hearing, the *Times-Union* published a cartoon of the hearing officer, characterizing him as a hanging judge who did not want to be confused with facts.

Shortly before the hearing, Mr. Davis and Sharon Lowry formed "People Who Care," an organization supporting the school board's removal of "textbooks containing filthy, vulgar language." The founders called for the switch from "Immoral, libertine courses to basics" and for the institution of "honest teacher evaluation." A reporter called Mel Gabler, one of the nation's most prominent textbook critics and a founder—with his wife—of Educational Research Analysts in Longview, Texas. The reporter wanted to determine whether the Gablers were involved in the Warsaw situation. After the reporter identified himself and before he could ask any questions, Mr. Gabler noted that Warsaw is a city in which good things are happening and "where we have the Lowrys and People Who Care."

13. Three months after the hearing, the hearing officer submitted his recommendation that the school board be ordered "to reverse all policies" noted in the original complaint to "status quo positions." The board announced that it would appeal the decision, but it did not have to do so. Two board members and two WCEA bargaining officials met in November and December to affect a compromise. The WCEA officials agreed to drop the hearing decision in return for the board's agreeing to the following:

a. to follow its own textbook review procedures in the future;
b. to write letters of explanation to the four transferred teachers;
c. to discuss possible curriculum changes with teachers before they are made;
d. to refrain from making major changes in working conditions without consulting the WCEA.

14. Two students and their parents filed suit in federal court, maintaining that the school board had violated constitutional guarantees of academic freedom and the students' "right to know." The district court dismissed the suit without trial, but the U.S. Court of Appeals for the Seventh Circuit ruled that a school board has the right to establish a curriculum on the basis of its own discretion; however, it is forbidden to impose a "pall of orthodoxy" on the classroom. The court recognized the right of students to file legal complaints about the school curriculum; however, the court held that the claims of the students "must cross a relatively high threshold before entering upon the field of a constitutional claim suitable for federal litigation."[2]

Secular humanism allegedly invaded the Ohio River town of Tell City during the 1981-82 academic year. Known for the manufacture of fine furniture, the peaceful community was split by a minister's declaration that the high school's English department was teaching "garbage" and that Christians in the community "need to take a stand against Satan's attack upon the minds of our youth."[3]

Tell City's winter of discontent began shortly after Thanksgiving when a ninth grader showed his mother several passages in John Steinbeck's *Of Mice and Men* and told her that he did not want to read the book as part of his English class assignment. Upon hearing the complaint of the mother, the English teacher said that her son could read Stephen Crane's *Red Badge of Courage* as independent reading while the rest of the class read Steinbeck. She and her son accepted the alternative assignment, and later she told the media that the English teacher treated her very well. But the mother also talked with her minister about the novel. The Reverend Don Reynolds, pastor of the Abundant Life Christian Church, had just opened a Christian school in Tell City. He expressed his displeasure with the literature assignment, with the Tell City schools in general, and with the English department in the high school in particular.

After telling his congregation about the "evil" novel, he and another minister prepared a petition to be presented to the school board. At the January board meeting, a group of 10 demanded that books "containing profanity and suggestive remarks" not be used in the schools. Then the minister from nearby Hawesville, Kentucky, who was acting as spokesperson for the group, accused the school board of being "anti-God." That evening marked the beginning of a three-month schoolbook protest that brought television cameras, nationally prominent textbook protesters, and divisiveness to Tell City.

Shortly after the mother complained about the Steinbeck novel, members of the school board discovered that they had never formally adopted their four-year-old policy for handling complaints about teaching materials. So the five-member board voted unanimously to make the policy official.

No one filed an official complaint against the novel. Nor did anyone sign a complaint form about *Finding My Way*, a textbook used in an elective sex education course for seventh and eighth graders. Instead, a small group led by a minister from a neighboring state protested the teaching of both books at the January meeting of the school board and used the local radio station and newspaper to condemn the books and the school system.

Several days after the January meeting of the board, the Reverend Steve Epley of Kentucky, writing a guest column for the Tell City *News,* raised the specter of secular humanism with these words:

> I am very much concerned about the humanist teachings in our public schools.
> What is Humanism? It is religion without God. It is the condition of man as described in the Bible (Romans 1:28) ". . . they did not like to retain God in their knowledge . . . and the results are indeed tragic. . ."
> The humanist is more dangerous than the atheist. At least, an atheist will

come right out and say he doesn't believe in God. A humanist will say, "Yes, I believe there is a God, but . . . I also believe in evolution."

The atheist is like a rattlesnake. He will make some noises before he bites you. But the humanist is more like a boa constrictor. He will silently squeeze you to death with his Godless philosophies before you know what happened.

Thus, Tell City's teachers joined the ranks of thousands who have been charged with "preaching the religion of secular humanism" in public schools. And like many of the thousands, Tell City's teachers were unaware of the crimes they were allegedly committing against society. They did not attend a church called Secular Humanist—in fact, they could not find one in Indiana if they tried. They could not define the religion; nor could they state its major beliefs. Yet they stood accused of spreading some doctrine that their accusers could not define and that prompted one minister to call Tell City's teachers and administrators "pagans and heathens" on a radio program. Another minister called school board members and the superintendent "rotten, stinking hypocrites who are spreading the religion of humanism through sex education."

Not all members of the clergy in Tell City were unhappy with the schools nor believed the secular humanism charge. Early in the controversy, three Catholic priests and four Protestant ministers sent the superintendent a letter in which they expressed their support of the school system. Several civic groups and organizations did the same.

Shortly after the Reverend Epley denounced the humanists in Tell City, a small group of citizens began compiling objections to some of the materials used in the public schools. At the February meeting of the school board, the Reverend Reynolds condemned the school system for allowing students to play "Dungeons & Dragons" in classrooms. He questioned the educational value of the game and challenged it for having the players pray to gods for magical powers in violation of the Supreme Court decision prohibiting prayer in public schools.

Throughout the schoolbook controversy, Superintendent William Wilson patiently explained that "Dungeons & Dragons" is played in a noncredit minicourse by students who elect the class. He also explained—again and again throughout the protest—that no students are forced to take sex education; rather, they elect to take it and they must have parental permission to do so.

On February 16, the Reverend Reynolds announced that Mel Gabler, co-founder of Educational Research Analysts and one of the most prominent textbook critics in the nation, would appear at a rally at the National Guard Armory at the end of the month. Approximately 300 people, including the Indiana chairperson of Phyllis Schlafly's "Stop Textbook Censorship Committee," attended the rally. Reporters estimated that at least one-third of the audience was there to support the school system.

Mel Gabler attacked the religion of secular humanism, sex education, "Dungeons & Dragons," and textbooks in general. He cited many passages in textbooks—only one of which was used in Tell City—to reinforce his belief that many of today's textbooks are dangerous because they promote evolution, situation ethics, sex education, world citizenship, and socialism—all of which he believes are tenets of the religion of secular humanism. He accused the school system of teaching "frills not skills," and he stated emphatically that standardized test scores in Tell City had declined steadily.

The superintendent, school board members, teachers, and administrators refuted the charges of Mel Gabler and others during the March meeting of the school board. Test scores have risen—not declined—the audience was told, and evidence was offered to support that statement. The basics are stressed in regular academic courses; "Dungeons & Dragons" is played only in a non-credit, elective minicourse. The school authorities repeatedly said that no student is required to take sex education; parental consent is required before a student may take the elective course.

At the March meeting, Anthony Pappano, president of the school board, read a statement in which he charged the protesters with using questionable tactics to attack the books. According to the president, the school critics did not follow the procedures for objecting to books, rather, he charged that they used the mass media and the rally to distort the truth and to make false and libelous statements. He promised that future school board meetings would not be used "as a forum by self-righteous groups to promote their personal beliefs. There will be no further discussion by the board on the topic of censorship until all interested parties have followed the established procedures of this school corporation." Finally, Pappano warned that if the protesting group persisted in using its present tactics and if it continued to make false and libelous statements about the school system and its employees, "we are prepared to take any and all legal action necessary to defend the constitutional rights of individuals associated with the corporation, including the educational rights of our children."

At the rally in February, the Reverend Reynolds had promised the audience that he would bring Norma Gabler, Phyllis Schlafly, and Billy O'Hair to Tell City for more rallies. He did not do so. Rather, he closed his Christian academy and left the community. The teachers, administrators, and school board members returned to the task of providing a solid education for their students. But the events of the winter of '82 have not been forgotten, and the scars are slow to heal.

For more than a decade, secular humanism has been a major target of the school book protesters. But now that the courts have not looked favorably on the charge that the schools are preaching that religion,[4] the protesters have other religious targets. Those targets—globalism and the New Age—surfaced in the literature of the new religious right several years before the courts frowned on the secular humanism charge.

Two school corporations in Gibson County in southern Indiana were accused of advancing both the New Age and globalism during the 1987–88 academic year. Seven women, including three teachers from the East Gibson schools, declared that they found both religions in *Tactics for Thinking*, a critical thinking skills program published by the Association for Supervision and Curriculum Development.

The seven women denounced *Tactics*, the New Age, and globalism in school board meetings at East and North Gibson and in intense letters-to-the editor campaigns in several area newspapers. The group was far more successful in East Gibson than in North Gibson, where the superintendent, school board, school administrators, and teachers stood firmly behind *Tactics*. The program in North Gibson was also endorsed by the Chamber of Commerce, Partners in Education, the Community Advisory Council, and the Ministerial Association. Thus, it was not surprising that, at its meeting in early May of 1988, the North Gibson School Board voted 5 to 0 to keep *Tactics*.

East Gibson seemed to be the more vulnerable of the two school systems because three teachers joined the seven-member protest group and because the target seemed to be the superintendent as much as the thinking skills program. When he was appointed to the superintendency, he was instructed by the board to strengthen the curriculum. Several of his changes in both staff and curriculum proved to be unpopular with some teachers.

At the December meeting of the East Gibson school board, the leader of the protest group read an eight-page statement denouncing *Tactics*, the New Age, and globalism. In it she charged that *Tactics* used "the same technique" employed "by hypnotists" and that the technique is also used in mind control and in "New Age meditation."[5] Apparently the leader of the protesters believes that the New Age movement described by Marilyn Ferguson in *The Aquarian Conspiracy* has a single religion, pantheism, and that it plans to impose a one-world government on this planet. Globalism, a term that she used interchangeably with global education, apparently has the same goals—a one-world religion and one-world government.

At the March meeting of the school board, the seven women presented their 42-page "preliminary report taken from the supporting research of the *Tactics for Thinking* manual.'' In it they noted that "globalists" will accomplish their goals of imposing a one-world government and religion on this earth by being critical of the United States and by stressing the need "for a breakdown of ethnocentrism (nationalism) and a need for some form of world government.''

The seven women tied *Tactics* to globalism by noting that Robert Marzano, the senior author, "references *Megatrends* by John Naisbitt, who states 'The fact is we have outlived the historical usefulness of representative democracy and we all sense intuitively that it is obsolete.' '' The women then noted that, on the back cover of *Megatrends*, Naisbitt "received glowing endorsement from Alvin Toffler, author of *The Third Wave*, a new age book, and from Marilyn Ferguson, one of the world's most infamous new agers...'' Thus, to the seven women, at least, it is crystal clear that Marzano's *Tactics* should be considered a product of the New Age movement because he "references" Naisbitt, who is endorsed by "new agers.''

The school board scheduled a modified debate on *Tactics* as part of its May meeting. Ronald S. Brandt, executive editor of ASCD, and I were given 35 minutes to present a case for *Tactics* and to refute the arguments used by the protesters, who were also given 35 minutes. Then each side was given 15 minutes for rebuttal. (It must be noted here that neither Brandt nor I received travel funds or consulting fees from East Gibson. And we never asked for any.)

In his opening statement, Brandt noted the purpose of *Tactics*, expressed his faith in the author, and refuted the hypnotism charge. After complimenting the seven protesters for their thoroughness, he said: "Unfortunately they have apparently misunderstood the program and misinterpreted its intent. There is nothing mysterious or subversive about any of the tactics. Many of them, in fact, are well known to many capable adults who have discovered these things for themselves.''

Mr. Brandt concluded his remarks by noting that *Tactics* "has no relationship whatever to global education. *Tactics* neither favors nor opposes global education; it deals with completely different content. Neither is it intended to promote any form of government; that is not its purpose. We do believe, though, that by teaching individuals how to be responsible, how to organize and remember knowledge, and how to reason logically, *Tactics* will help children become better American Citizens.''

In the remainder of the 35 minutes, I focused primarily on the arguments the protest leader presented to the school board in December. I gave the members of the school board and the protesters my commentary on the eight-page presentation. I made 53 notes, 14 of which are several paragraphs long. Most of my notes challenged the facts and/or the evidence in the 29 paragraphs in the protest leader's statement.

71

I also distributed a two-page definition of global education by a prominent global educator. Then I compared the attacks on *Tactics* and global education to the strategies used against secular humanism, and I refuted the protesters' definitions of global education, attention control, and pantheism. I further noted that in reviewing the documents prepared by the seven women, I detected the direct influence of these five national organizations that attempt to remove materials from public schools: Eagle Forum, Concerned Women of America, National Association of Christian Educators, Citizens for Excellence in Education, and Educational Research Analysts. Through further investigation, I found materials that could be traced to the John Birch Society. My findings were not disputed in the protesters' rebuttal.

In their 35-minute presentation, the protesters read from their 42-page document. Then they used student actors to point out the similarities among yoga, self-hypnosis, involuntary attention, semitrances, and three exercises in *Tactics*.[6] They claimed that the three exercises could cause students to fall into trances without teachers realizing it. One of the exercises calls for students to stare at something, such as a spot on the wall, for about a minute and try to block all else from their minds. Then students are to tell what thoughts interfered with their concentration on the spot.

In the 15-minute rebuttal, Mr. Brandt disputed the charge that the three exercises constitute self-hypnotism. He also repeated his contention that *Tactics* has no connection with global education, globalism, or the New Age movement.

Former Indiana State Senator Joan Gubbins was the major spokesperson in the protesters' rebuttal. At that time she served as a member of the President's Committee on Education. She congratulated the seven women on their fine work and for their concern for the children in the community. Then she read selected passages from Marzano's own evaluation of the thinking skills program and concluded that it is a "a little oversold and grossly underinvestigated." Approximately 60 percent of the audience gave Senator Gubbins and her companions a standing ovation.

At the end of the modified debate, the president announced that the board would vote on *Tactics* at its June meeting. The board voted then, by a 3–2 margin, to let those teachers who were using *Tactics* to continue to do so. Response to the board action was immediate. Members of the audience jeered the resolutions and disrupted the remainder of the meeting. The protesters announced that they would recall one of the board members and denounced all three who voted for the resolutions. They declared that they would continue their fight against New Age globalistic programs they disliked and that they would elect their candidates to the school board. One segment of the audience sang "God Bless America" loudly and the president adjourned the board meeting before business was completed.

Two months later the board reversed its decision and eliminated *Tactics*. By that time the superintendent had resigned to accept a superintendency with a larger corporation. A reporter for a newspaper in the northern part of Indiana revealed that, during his final year at East Gibson, the superintendent's family suffered harassment and he endured threats.

The Gibson County struggle goes on. Apparently it will continue until the protesters are satisfied that the New Age movement and globalism are no longer in the schools.

LESSONS TO BE LEARNED IN PREPARATION FOR THE SCHOOLBOOK PROTESTERS

The three incidents are most instructive. An analysis of the three, as well as many other incidents I have studied, yields these major lessons:

1. Teachers should select materials that are consistent with the educational objectives of the school system and of specific courses. When controversial materials are appropriate for specific courses—and they frequently are—teachers might want to prepare written rationales for the use of those materials in case they are challenged. (It should be noted that recent court cases have proved that virtually anything, including basal readers, can be labeled controversial by some individual and groups.)

2. Teachers should be ready to make alternative assignments when they have their classes study novels or other supplementary materials. They should make certain that any student who requests an alternative assignment is not made to feel like an outcast.

3. Every school system must have written materials selection policies that include procedures for handling complaints. The policies and procedures should be readily available, and they should be followed to the letter by everyone connected with the school system. No one should be able to act unilaterally to remove a book, course, film, or teaching method. (Materials selection policies and procedures for reviewing challenged materials are available from nearly every major professional organization.)

When materials are challenged—whether the challenge comes from a board member, a parent, a teacher, a student, or an administrator—the challenged material should be given to the duly authorized reconsideration committee for its recommendation. No action should be taken on

73

any teaching material or method until after the reconsideration committee examines the work, course syllabus, or teaching method.

If a teacher or librarian is accused of teaching or disseminating "objectionable" material, that person should be fully apprised of the charge at the earliest possible moment. Teachers and librarians throughout the nation have told me that they have effectively warded off a full-blown protest by having the opportunity to talk—informally and amicably—to the person who is considering the possibility of making a challenge. Teachers tell me that many parents simply want to know how a book is treated or why a teacher has made a specific selection. Teachers indicate that they must not be too quick to haul out the complaint form and insist that it be completed. An informal discussion may solve a problem.

4. Teachers and administrators must know as much as possible about the secular humanism, New Age, and globalism charges. They cannot take the charges lightly because protesters have used them effectively in some communities to rid the schools of books, courses, films, and teaching methods. Teachers must become familiar with court decisions about secular humanism, keeping in mind that the New Age charges may be taken through the courts before they, too, are less threatening. School officials must not respond hastily to the charge that courses and books reflect the religion of the New Age movement. Critics must prove that there is a single New Age religion and that it is the religion of the public schools. That charge will be extremely difficult to prove, just as it is difficult to prove that secular humanism is, indeed, a religion and that it is the religion of the public schools.

5. Trial by newspaper has become common in schoolbook protest incidents. Protesters have discovered that the letters-to-the-editor columns in area newspapers and radio call-in programs are effective vehicles for attacking anything they do not like. Therefore, school systems and local teacher organizations must demand equal time or space for responsible rebuttals.

6. School boards should have a policy in which they state that petitions will not be taken seriously if they contain names of persons not in the community. School boards should also have someone verify the names.

7. Anyone who has a complaint about a school system or any of its teaching materials deserves a fair and courteous hearing. However, teachers and administrators have every right to point out distortions or errors in fact. After a fair exchange of charges and responses, a school system must make certain that unfounded criticism and/or libelous statements

do not interfere with the school's most important task—educating the young.

8. A school board should never give up its legal rights. Citizen pressure groups have a right to express their views to the board. But that does not mean that their views should dictate—or take precedence over—board policy.

9. All school personnel should become familiar with the goals, tactics, and literature of the major school protest groups in this country. Teachers and administrators should have more than a nodding acquaintance with materials prepared by Eagle Forum, Concerned Women of America, Citizens for Excellence in Education, National Association of Christian Educators, and Educational Research Analysts—among others.

10. Students should not be isolated from the controversy. In both Warsaw and Tell City, students expressed their concern about the removal of materials and made every attempt to protect their rights. Students stood firmly behind the school board, superintendent, and teachers in Tell City. That united front is imperative.

NOTES

1. Full documentation of the Warsaw story appears in Chapter 1 of Edward B. Jenkinson's *Censors in the Classroom: The Mind Benders* (Carbondale, Ill.: Southern Illinois University Press, 1979). Facts are taken from minutes of school board meetings, newspaper clippings, and personal interviews of the participants in the incidents. I spent more than 20 days in Warsaw, studying the censorship incident.

2. *Zykan v. Warsaw Community School Corporation and Warsaw School Board of Trustees*, 631 F.2d 1300 (7th Cir. 1980).

3. Full documentation appears in Edward B. Jenkinson, *The Tale of Tell City: An Anti-Censorship Saga* (Washington, D.C.: People for the American Way, 1983), and in Edward B. Jenkinson, *The Schoolbook Protest Movement: 40 Questions & Answers* (Bloomington, Ind.: Phi Delta Kappa Educational Foundation, 1986). Facts are taken from minutes of school board meetings, newspaper clippings, tapes of the rally and of school board meetings, and interviews with the superintendent.

4. See *Grove v. Mead School District No. 354*, 753 F.2d 1528 (1985); *Mozert v. Hawkins County Board of Education*, 827 F.2d 1058 (1987); and *Smith v. Board of School Commissioners of Mobile County*, 827 F.2d 684 (1987).

5. Presentation of Jeanne Georges to the School Board of the East Gibson School Corporation, December 14, 1987. Documentation for the Gibson County incident appears in articles by Edward Jenkinson that were published in *Phi Delta Kappan* (September 1988), *Educational Leadership* (October 1988), and *Newsletter on Intellectual Freedom* (December 1988). Facts are taken from minutes of school board meetings, newspaper clippings, interviews with the Gibson County superintendents, and documents by the protesters.

6. According to the protesters, three exercises in *Tactics* could cause students to fall into self-hypnotic trances. The first suggests to teachers that they have students "focus their attention on some stimulus (e.g., a spot on the wall). Explain to them that you want them to focus all of their energy for about a minute and ask them to be aware of what it is like when they are really trying to attend to something." The second exercise suggests that teachers have students focus their attention on a stimulus again, only this time students are asked to "identify the physical characteristics they associate with raising their energy level (e.g., sit up straight, raise your head off your neck)." The third exercise: "Have students practice the attention control process periodically throughout the day."

APPENDIX

by Janet L. Jones

The material in this section was prepared by Janet L. Jones for the Washington Education Association's resource manual, *What's Left After the Right?*

Dr. Jones has been a public school educator since 1970. She has been a teacher, counselor, vice principal, district director of guidance, and curriculum specialist. She is a staff member of the graduate school, Counseling Psychology Department at Lewis and Clark College in Portland, Oregon, and also directs her own consulting firm, Education Consulting Service. The following sections are from the manual:

1. The Typical Censorship Scenario (p. 22)
2. Six Case Studies with Helpful Tips (pp. 109–18)
3. Countering Far Right Tactics (pp. 121–23)
4. Generic Materials Selection (pp. 170–75)
5. Survival Tips (pp. 176–81)

1. THE TYPICAL CENSORSHIP SCENARIO

Following are the usual incidents that occur when a curriculum controversy escalates and the school personnel are unsuccessful in thwarting the barrage of allegations and rhetoric.

1. A district administrator or teacher receives an initial complaint by phone, a visit or a letter.
2. Informal attempts to resolve the concern are not successful.
3. A group of concerned citizens appear at a board meeting to express complaints and give demands. Often they are armed with legal quotes, pamphlets, video cameras and prepared rhetorical statements.
4. Letters to the editor begin appearing in the local newspaper.
5. Flyers or notices are distributed throughout the community containing complaints, allegations, charges, etc.
6. Community meetings begin and at times feature guest speakers from regional or national Religious Right organizations. Anti-public education literature and films are often used.
7. Board meetings become stages for hostile confrontations.
8. Newspapers and television coverage mounts, initiated and sustained most often by the ultra-conservative activists.
9. Certain administrators, teachers, or board members are singled out as the ultimate villains.
10. Materials Review Committee members receive intimidating phone calls and letters.
11. Board recall petitions are circulated.
12. Law suits are threatened (often initiated from both camps).
13. School funding elections are not supported.
14. Legal fees for the district accelerate.
15. New school board candidates, representing the Far Right philosophy, surface and are often supported by outside funds.
16. The confrontation recycles for about three years as new topics and issues are challenged.

Unless effective action is taken:

- Educational programs lose their momentum.
- Random, persistent charges will continue to undermine staff effectiveness and trust.
- School-community relationships begin to deteriorate.
- Frustrations and hostilities are manifested inwardly toward self or other staff members.
- Some staff will leave the district.
- Educators self-censor to avoid any more conflicts.
- The school board becomes a mouthpiece and power base for the Righteous Right.

2. SIX CASE STUDIES WITH HELPFUL TIPS

Situation #1

Meetings, mailings, letters to the editor, talk shows, etc., have become the focal points of an ultra-conservative group in your community.

This group is promoting a negative, anti-public education campaign and is focusing on the following issues:

1. Your district has been using federal monies to illegally buy secular humanistic classroom materials, thus violating the Hatch Amendment.
2. The district has homosexuals on the staff and the Far Right group wants the "perverts" to be identified and immediately fired. (Issue is referenced as a violation of the parents' and students' First Amendment rights.)

A representative from the "Concerned Women for America" is coming to address your board in one week, at which time she will demand the district show just cause as to why they have not immediately responded to the wishes of the taxpayers. Your board wants ideas, help and a proactive response from administrators, teachers, and classified personnel.

Questions:

1. As a *teacher*, how would you advise your board?
2. As an *administrator*, what specific ideas will you offer?
3. As a *classified employee*, what advice from your perspective will you give to the board?
4. Are there legal, moral, and ethical violations involved in these demands? If so, what are they, from your perspective?
5. How may the responses to this scenario be focused on developing a proactive stance?

Some Helpful Tips

The following tips constitute some basic ideas that you may want to consider as you process the scenario:

1. Request clarification from the complainants, in writing, of their definition of secular humanism and exactly which federal grant the district is allegedly misusing.
2. Obtain copies of the Hatch Amendment and have someone at the board meeting who can clarify this law.

3. Obtain copies of any statutes and collective bargaining agreement language that relate to individuals' rights in the workplace.
4. Locate and have available any district policy and procedures relative to personnel rights and protections.
5. Advise the complainants that free-floating accusations cannot be tolerated and legal action against them may be a consequence.
6. Have copies of the First Amendment available as a reference for board members, staff, parents, and citizens.

A proactive stance would most likely include:

1. Expressing empathy for the complainants' concerns.
2. Demonstrating that district officials are well informed about the federal/state laws and district policies and procedures.
3. Clarifying in calm, precise language what laws and policies allow or do not allow and that the district is adhering to those precepts by doing the following:

---

4. Remembering the pitfalls of getting caught up in emotionally-ridden allegations and instead focusing constantly on law, policy, procedures, and specifics.
5. Allowing the complainants an opportunity to reconsider their demands or to offer other suggestions based on the parameters of law and policy. (In other words, provide a graceful way out for the complainants.)
6. Making sure the press has a full report of the allegations and exactly how the district responsibly resolved the issue.

Situation #2

The library assistant comes to you regarding a set of books called *Inner City Nursery Rhymes*. These are in the primary level library. She wants them out now! You look quickly through one of the books and agree the content does have some explicit profanity.

These books had gone through the district procedure for library materials purchases two years ago. The librarian has checked and the other elementary school in your district has two of these books also.

You know the assistant, Miss Ima Reader, belongs to the local Eagle Forum group. Your district has just completed a long and hostile series of hearings on the use of guidance activities in the classroom. The resolution of these hearings was to keep the materials, but allow students to opt out of the health-guidance units. No one seemed to like the solution

81

and school-community-staff relations are already uneasy and strained.

Your answers to the following questions should be based on your position as teacher, board member or administrator.

Questions:

1. What are you going to tell the library assistant right now? (Remember, in this case study you are to think about being in the position of agreeing, somewhat, with the library assistant. In other words, how will you respond when you support academic freedom and the right to read, but find yourself offended, personally and professionally by this material?)
2. Who else in your district/building needs to be informed and/or involved?
3. What should you know about your district's policies and procedures to accurately advise this person?

Some Helpful Tips

Research indicates that approximately 30 percent of the complaints filed against curricular or instructional materials, come from within the educational ranks. Further, as more and more of these kind of incidents occur, it has been shown through data collection and information sharing among districts, that it becomes easier and easier to simply take a book off the shelf. Once a district has experienced a curricular controversy educators may well be tempted to avoid defending other controversial topics simply to avoid the turmoil, trauma and time consumption.

So with Ms. Ima Reader, the following tips may be helpful:

1. Let the complainant know that you have heard the concern and that you will assist every way you can to have the issue addressed quickly, fairly and according to district policies.
2. Refer Miss Reader to the district's policy and procedure for reconsideration of controversial materials.
3. Explain that the concern must be submitted in writing. (Your district's policy should require this!)
4. Do not suggest the book be removed from the shelf today! (Removing the book right now really implies permission for self-censorship to occur anytime, by any person.)
5. Inform the building and central office administration, or whomever the district has (or should have) designated as the one responsible for handling curricular controversy issues.
6. Initiate or request initiation of the process for reconsideration of materials. Because the book "appears" (in your opinion) to be in-

appropriate, speed up the process, **but ALWAYS follow the process.**

7. No matter if you are a teacher, an administrator, a board member or the custodian, take time to re-familiarize yourself with the appropriate and related district policies.

We may not resolve the person's exact demand on the spot, but we can, and always should listen to the concern and assure that the "proper" steps will be taken, as quickly as possible.

Situation #3

Five parents walk into your building, and without clearance through the school office, go down the hall into the third grade classroom. They begin ripping down the bulletin board and wall displays of the witches, black cats, the fake cobwebs and ghosts made of sheets that are suspended on wires from the ceiling.

The children sit in amazement as the parents snatch things from the walls. The teacher attempts to discuss the issue and to calm the swarm but they just ignore her. They stuff the spoils into shopping bags and march out.

As they leave, they stop by the office to show the evidence they have collected to be used against the principal, the teacher, and the district. They intend to file a legal claim that the school has blatantly ignored the Constitution of the United States. Their contention is, that the teacher has violated the First Amendment regarding the separation of church and state because she was teaching the religion of Satanism and celebrating the "unholy" religious holiday of witches, called All Hallow's Eve.

Neighboring districts have had very long, painful, and expensive experiences with similar groups. Your district has talked about doing something, but nothing has really been put in place.

Questions:

1. If you were that teacher, what would you have done?
2. What rights of access to classrooms do parents legally have?
3. What are some of the first steps this district needs to do to become better prepared for the apparent onslaught?

Some Helpful Tips

The district should have policies and procedures related to persons entering school property and classrooms. These regulations, for the most part are put ito place as a means to protect students and staff from those persons who have "questionable" cause to be on school grounds. Persons not so welcome may include drug dealers, gang members, etc. District policies and various state statutes should include some guidance, however, regarding the entrance of parents or patrons onto school property. We would like to believe that everyone who enters a school building would have the best interests of the children at heart. And, while the parents who entered this third grade classroom sincerely believed they had the best interests of those students at heart, they did inappropriately impose their own beliefs and actions on the children and teacher.

For purposes of discussion, the following ideas may be considered:

1. The teacher, of course, would ask the parents to cease and desist, and immediately notify the administrator. Never try to stop them physically.
2. After the parents march out, the teacher has to remain calm, and to her best ability help the students understand what had just happened.
3. The administrator needs to get the names of the parents involved.
4. If possible, and if time warrants, give the parents any district policies or information regarding holiday celebrations.
5. Advise the appropriate central office department of the incident.
6. Gather data about church-state and legal issues from existing policies, the district's legal counsel, the appropriate office of the state department of education, professional organizations, and/or consultants.
7. Inform and educate the board of the incident, the legal issues involved and the relationship of this incident to the overall agenda of the Far Right movement.
8. Inform the media, and include what the district is doing to address the parents' concerns according to legal precedence and district policy. Avoid emotionalism and allegations.

Situation #4

The Thespian Club in your district has been working for weeks on their production of *Of Mice and Men*. The first production is scheduled for tonight. It is one o'clock in the afternoon and the drama coach roars down the hall yelling that the superintendent just called her and informed her that:

1. A parent had complained about the profanity in the play.
2. He, the superintendent, wanted all the cussing removed from the play, immediately, or it was to be cancelled.
3. If she let the play go on as originally written, she would be insubordinate.

The teacher is threatening to make calls, right now, to the press and the American Civil Liberties Union (ACLU). There is a controversial issues policy for the district. The drama coach has not gotten approval to do the play through this process. The policy, however, does not address student productions.

Your five-member board has three ultra-conservative representatives on it and these three people swayed the vote to hire the present superintendent.

Questions:

1. If you were the drama coach, would you make the students delete all expletives before the show?
2. From your perspective as a colleague, association representative, or administrator, what kinds of power and political issues need to be considered?
3. What does the district need to do to prevent this kind of situation from happening again?

Some Helpful Tips

There are several issues involved in this scenario, some of which have no specific answer. Each district has its own climate and structure. Sometimes this climate allows for challenge and innovation and at times it does not. Further, the depth of your own value structure and beliefs will determine your course of action.

Following are some ideas to consider regarding your particular situation as they relate to this scenario:

1. The decision to delete or not delete the profanity from the play depends on a variety of issues. Even though very frustrated and angry, the teacher should refer to the district's policies on controversial issues, seek advice immediately from the Education Association representative and if warranted , talk to legal counsel.
2. Right now, give some thought to just how much do you value academic freedom and, to what extent are you willing to defend it.
3. Districts not only need policies regarding the selection of materials, but they need policies and procedures for the internal processes of removal and appeal.
4. Board-approved Academic Freedom Statements are extremely important. (Note the ''Resource and Materials'' section of this manual for examples.) These can provide protection against and help eliminate last minute dictates.
5. Always take a few minutes to check policy and procedure before taking on a project that may be controversial.

6. If you are in a position where you feel powerless, no reasonable policies regarding academic freedom exist and the politics of the system do not reflect your beliefs, then you have some very serious thinking to do about your options, which may include:
   a. Organizing a core of colleagues/citizens to work within the system to initiate positive changes (Refer to the Action Plan Examples on pages 159 and 160 [of the manual] for some creative ideas)
   b. Ignoring the situation
   c. Openly resisting the system
   d. Sabotaging the system (you usually lose this one)
   e. Leaving the district.

Situation #5

A group of citizens has notified the superintendent's secretary that they will all be present at the next board of directors' meeting that will be held two weeks from now. The grapevine reveals that this group is bringing in outside "scholars" to present their case regarding equal time for creationism in the high school biology classes.

You are a member of the district curriculum selection team and therefore, your superintendent has asked all of you to become involved. He wants you at this particular board meeting to provide a "constructive" response to the citizen group.

Your district has never faced a major censorship or curricular controversy. Yet, you know that the current board of directors leans to the conservative, but not a radically conservative orientation. Districts nearby have been increasingly bombarded with materials from the profamily forum and other religious right groups. The surface appears calm but you sense a tsunami is forming.

Questions:

1. How will the committee go about determining the legality and appropriateness of the request?
2. Just what is a "conservative" response?
3. What can you do in two weeks time? And, who all could/should be involved?
4. What do you foresee for long-range strategies?

Some Helpful Tips

The issue of creationism is a time-worn issue that still creates emotional havoc among community members and the schools. There are, however, resources to which you may refer illustrating how the topic may be handled.

Following are some ideas that you may find useful:

1. As always, check to see if the district has any existing policies and procedures regarding creationism and/or teaching about religion.
2. If not, begin calling neighboring districts, the state department of education and professional organizations to collect sample policies, legal referents, curricular ideas, etc.
3. Make a decision about the legality of the request.
4. Try to determine how many people support the addition of creationism to the curriculum. (Are we looking at a small core of people or does the requesting group represent a large segment of the community?)
5. Your committee's constructive response might include the following:
   a. A statement of appreciation for the concerns of parents who initiated the request;
   b. The legality of the issue of teaching creationism based on case precedence/law in your state;
   c. A description of what the state requires for instruction in high school biology classes;
   d. A description of what is currently being taught in the biology classes;
   e. A suggestion that a study group be formed to investigate creative solutions that are consistent with the law and policy.

   Note: You may want to find out how many churches in the community are teaching creationism to school-age children. This information may be helpful to make the point that those children whose parents want them to learn this belief are already receiving excellent instruction from their respective churches.

6. You may want to consider adding some community people to your Curriculum Selection Committee, particularly someone from the local ministerial association.

Situation #6

Several districts in the state (and you've heard about some nationally) have experienced very serious curricular challenges to their critical thinking programs. Most specifically challenged have been "talented" and "gifted" programs, and a particular curricuum titled *Techniques*. This program incudes deep thinking and the use of the Socratic Method of reasoning and visualization. From what you have read, you have some concerns about critical-thinking-type programs.

An administrative committee in your district reviewed the *Techniques* curriculum and decided tht all teachers would be required to implement it in their classrooms. And, the district expects a resultant improvement on the students' achievement test scores for the forthcoming year.

You do not like the newly adopted *Techniques* curriculum. You are not particularly happy about how the district "decided" that everyone has to teach critical thinking, and further, you do not feel you have the skills or preparation to teach "deep thinking" or those other New Age methodologies. In fact, you really think that critical thinking lessons very often encroach on parents' rights to teach their own children appropriate morals, values, and traditonal choices for life.

Questions:

1. What options can you pursue if what you are asked to teach significantly violates your beliefs?
2. How might you help/advise a colleague who quietly self-censors materials to avoid teaching the required curriculum?
3. Is self-censorship ever appropriate for public educators?

Some Helpful Tips

This example may well stimulate the most active discussion of all the scenarios! As in some of the preceding examples, there are no clear-cut answers that will or can apply to everyone. It is hoped, however, that those of us in the teaching profession can find innovative ways to balance our beliefs with the pressures, expectations and laws under which we must perform our jobs.

The following ideas are offered to further stimulate discussion and hopefully will not muddy the waters even more:

1. If you are asked to teach something that clearly violates your values, your options are to check your contract for stipulations, limitations and expectations. Contact your association representative for information and ideas.
2. Take your case to the appropriate administrator with alternative suggestions and recommendations, e.g., your switching classes with another teacher; providing an alternate course or unit; having a guest instructor for that particular topic; your teaching another teacher's class during that specific unit, while they teach the unit that disturbs you.
3. If a teacher is self-censoring his or her curriculum you could consider talking to them privately to see if there are ways to help them or if you can assist with the suggestion of alternatives.

4. Recommend inservice training for staff to be conducted by outside consultants, curriculum experts or staff membes who have expertise in the new curricular area.
5. Weigh the necessity for this particular job against what the job requires. While quiet, self-censorship often relieves us from doing that which we dislike, it most frequently results in our having to wrestle with our conscience and professional ethics. This is a very difficult and personal issue requiring much thought and care.

3. COUNTERING FAR RIGHT TACTICS

Responding to the charges and allegations of Far Right proponents can be an extremely emotional and frustrating experience. The Human and Civil Rights Division of the National Education Association has developed an excellent list of suggestions that are helpful in the event you are directly involved in a confrontation. Following are adaptations of that list plus some additional ideas.

- Challenge the credibility of the attacking group by identifying and calling attention to the misrepresentations, generalizations, half-truths, etc., in their arguments.
- Attempt to resolve confusion regarding misstatements about public education, the school district, a particular book or curricular program through clarification and examples.
- Avoid giving legitimacy and emphasis to Far Right charges or their sources.

Inappropriate Responses

Responses that never work for you and most often work against you:

1. Denial (flat out) of the charge without explanation, factual evidence, substantive data, law, etc.
   Example: "Our district would never do that."
2. Personal attacks or making unsubstantiated charges.
   Example: "You're obviously one of those holy rollers with an axe to grind against the schools."
3. Use of defensive statements or giving reasons for district action or decisions that are not really justified.
   Example: "That's true, but we had to buy those materials because they were on the text list and neighboring districts bought them."

Avoiding Critical Confrontations

1. Be prepared. Have, readily at hand, facts, policies, statutes, district goal statements, minutes of meetings, state mandates, etc.
2. Identify the source or supplier of materials used by your opponent. Let the community know who the major supporter, developer or promoter is and what they have to gain from the challenge.
3. Use humor, cautiously and wisely. Only use humor very selectively and carefully. It can easily backfire or come back to haunt you later. One comment taken from context can be made to have a whole new meaning.

4. Expose critics' tactics immediately! Use specific examples and data to let the community know exactly how the truth is being stretched, misused, taken from context or is an exact replica of materials from Far Right groups.
5. Use the public forum to educate your public and to demonstrate professional control, experience and assertiveness. Anticipate the charges and tactics and move smoothly around them or use them to your advantage.
6. Become familiar with the language and rhetoric of Far Right groups, for example:
   - Answering questions with questions
   - Not answering your question but moving to topics of their choice
   - Using broad generalizations
   - Making sweeping generalizations about historical precedence that appeal to patriotism and family tradition
   - Claiming Constitutional rights beyond those given or implied
   - Quoting legal decisions that are not correct or only partially apply to the given situation
   - Attempting to intimidate school personnel through use of VCR tapings
   - Threatening budget failures
   - Loading audiences with their specific supporters
   - Questioning the certification and professional qualifications of district administrators and teachers
   - Threatening to recall board members
   - Bringing prepared policy statements to counter ones in existence in the district
   - Asking administrators to quote statute or administrative rule numbers on the spot
   - Providing evidence from "authoritative" sources
   - Giving new definitions for educational terms and demanding administrators to defend or deny those definitions
   - Always getting the last word (even if it has to be shouted) before leaving a meeting.
7. Respond professionally to all concerns. Do not become guilty of categorizing all complaints as emanating from parents whose thoughts and energies are manipulated by Religious Right organizations. The fear experienced by concerned parents is real and must be dealt with professionally and sincerely.
8. Be familiar with Far Right leaders, organizations, publications, and tactics, before your district is confronted.
9. Analyze and get to know your community. Make friends with your neighbors. Build allies and strengthen bonds.

10. Identify other individuals and groups that have something to lose by the encroachment of the Far Right philosophy into the community and school system (e.g., libraries, mainline religions, local radio and television, some women's groups, academic organizations, labor unions, etc.).
11. Keep the public informed about treasured rights and the freedoms to learn, think, question, make decisions, disagree and be different.
12. Celebrate, promote and extol teachers and public education with more vigor, creativity and enthusiasm than ever before.
13. Develop lines of communication among staff to keep them informed and involved. Make this a priority. Set up a hot line if necessary. Nip rumors in the bud.

4. GENERIC MATERIALS SELECTION AND RECONSIDERATION POLICY GUIDE

The following outline is meant to serve only as one of several references that could be considered when drafting or rewriting policy.

Instruction

The board is legally reponsible for the selection of all instructional materials used in the district. The responsibility for preparing all student reading lists and for examining, evaluating and selecting all supplementary materials is delegated to the professional staff of the district.

The collective bargaining agreement of _____ School District (dated ____) defines, incorporates and assures academic freedom for staff and students.

1.0 Purpose of Instructional Materials

    1.1 Instructional materials shall enrich and support the curriculum, taking into consideration the varied instructional needs, abilities, interests and maturity levels of the students.

    1.2 Instructional materials shall stimulate student growth in conceptual thinking, factual knowledge, physical fitness, literary appreciation, esthetic values and the development of ethical standards.

    1.3 Instructional materials shall be of sufficient variety so as to present opposing views of controversial issues in order that young citizens may develop the skills of critical analysis and informed decision making.

    1.4 Instructional materials shall contribute to the development of an understanding of the ethnic, cultural and occupational diversity of American life.

    1.5 Instructional materials including textbooks, programmed learning, telecourses, packaged courses or units, filmed courses and the like are generally the basic resources for teaching and learning. Therefore all of the above criteria must be adhered to in their selection.

2.0 Selection and Adoption Process

    2.1 Basic textbooks for each course and/or grade level shall be selected according to state code (law, statute, ordinance, etc.) _____, and the applicable regulations of the Office of the Superintendent of Public Instruction and the state Board of Education.

2.2 The selection of basic materials for schools of the district is delegated to the professionally trained personnel employed by the district and is subject to review by the Instructional Materials Committee and ultimate approval by the local school board.

2.3 The district's professionally trained staff has the responsibility of assuring that instructional materials are used at appropriate grade or instructional levels.

2.4 Additional instructional materials may be selected by individual teachers for occasional use in the classroom. Such materials are to be relevant to the content of the course and to the purpose of the school system.

2.5 The authority to prepare recommended lists of supplementary materials used by students in a particular class, media center or department, in addition to the basic texts is vested in the classroom teachers and or media specialists. Such lists will be prepared in the context of a particular instructional program and presented to the building principal for his/her information.

2.6 Upon approval by the Instructional Materials Committee (IMC) a teacher may initiate trial use of a textbook or other instructional materials for up to one full school year before adoption by the board.

2.7 Books and other instructional materials donated to the district shall be reviewed by the Instructional Materials Committee and shall not be included in the curriculum unless and until approved by such committee pursuant to its selection criteria.

2.8 Persons wishing to review materials may do so by appointment, during normal office hours. The review process must not (a) interfere with the teacher's ability to perform his/her duties or (b) interfere with the teacher's ability to use the materials.

3.0 Instructional Materials Committee

3.1 Membership: The Instructional Materials Committee shall consist of the following (examples of varying constituencies are listed below):
- One elementary and one secondary principal;
- One elementary and one secondary teacher;
- Two volunteer citizens;
- The curriculum administrator;
  (or)
- Three teachers and two citizens chosen by the local teachers' association;
- Three administrators;
- One citizen selected by the board;

3.2 Terms of Office

Members are appointed by _____ (superintendent, the board, etc.) for a three year term.

3.3 Responsibilities of the committee:

3.31 A committee chairperson shall be selected from among the committee members to serve for one year.

3.32 Committee chair responsiblities shall be:
- Schedule regular meetings;
- Preside at all meetings;
- Cause a written record to be maintained for all meetings and decisions;
- Appoint ad hoc committees as needed and as approved by the total committee and the superintendent.

3.33 Committee duties shall be limited to:
- Reviewing instructional materials that have been recommended by teacher selection teams to determine:
  - If curriculum adoption processes have been followed:
  - If federal, state laws have been met;
  - If stated goals and objectives of the district have been met;
- Reviewing annually with the administrator responsible for district curriculum, the criteria, timelines and methods used for the selection of instructional materials, including supplemental materials;
- Reviewing challenged materials and submitting recommendations to the superintendent.

3.34 Routine materials selection procedures:
- If the committee supports the proposed materials, an acceptance letter will be drawn and forwarded to the superintendent who will present the recommendation to the board.
- If the IMC rejects the proposed adoption, they will return the materials to the initiators with a written proposal containing suggestions, alternatives and timelines for further action.

4.0 Procedures for Processing Complaints Regarding Instructional Materials

4.1 When a complaint is received from a resident or employee of the district regarding instructional materials in a specific school the teacher, media specialist and the principal ("building personnel") shall be notified of the complaint and its source.

If building personnel agree that the disputed material should be retained, the complainant will be contacted in an attempt to resolve the issue. If the complainant continues to dispute the material, the principal shall assist the complainant in completing a Request for Reconsideration Form and forward this form to the superintendent (or designee). The principal will notify the chairperson of the IMC of the forthcoming complaint.

If building personnel cannot reach agreement among themselves, or if they concur that the material should be removed, they will immediately notify the superintendent (or designee), who in turn will notify the IMC committee.

4.2 When notified that (a) building personnel concur in the removal of disputed material, (b) building personnel disagree about the propriety of disputed material, or (c) a Request for Reconsideration Form has been filed, the superintendent (designee) shall:

Following are two options to consider at this point:

1. The IMC hears testimony from all concerned in an open hearing and submits recommendations to the superintendent and the board, or
2. The IMC hears testimony from the complainant and involved professional staff in a closed session and submits recommendations to the superintendent and the board.

IMC Open Hearing Option

4.21 Set a time and place for an open hearing by the IMC. Such hearing shall be held within 20 calendar days of notification of the superintendent by his/her receipt of the Reconsideration Form.

4.22 Notify the complainant, appropriate staff members, including teachers using the materials, and local media of the time and place of the hearing. Such notification shall include an invitation to present relevant information. Notification will include time limits for presentations, procedures that will be used and protocol guidelines for the hearing.

4.23 Assemble such data including reviews and professional opinions of the materials, teacher perspectives, the specific objections of the complainant, for the IMC to properly perform its function.

4.24 Decisions of the committee shall be delivered to the complainant, the superintendent, media and affected building personnel in writing within 20 calendar days of the hearing.

4.25 If the committee does not find in favor of the complainant, the complainant will be notified in writing of his/her right to appeal the decision to the school board within 30 days of receipt of the notice.

4.26 Any staff member, particularly those staff members whose instructional materials were/are the subject of the complaint and who believe the decision of the IMC warrants further consideration, may also file for an appeal, to the board, within thirty (30) days.

4.27 If the board concurs with the IMC's recommendation(s), that decision is final.

4.28 If the board does not agree with the recommendation(s) of the IMC, the board shall return the IMC recommendation and a written statement explaining the board's reasons for rejecting the committee's position.

4.29 The IMC will have 15 calendar days to reconsider its initial recommendation(s) as well as the board's written reasons for rejection.

4.30 The second IMC decision shall be delivered in writing to the board within the 10 calendar days.

4.31 The board will issue its final decision to involved staff and citizens within 30 calendar days.

4.32 Any disputed material will remain in use in school system pending final resolution.

4.33 If a parent requests in writing that his/her student not use the questioned material, the student will be given the opportunity, under the direction and recommendation of the teacher, to use alternative materials.

IMC Closed Hearing Option

4.21 The IMC is convened by the chairperson and the committee will reevaluate the material giving full consideration to state and district educational objectives.

4.22 The committee will request the complainant and the person(s) primarily responsible for the use of the material, to appear before the IMC to offer additional information concerning the complaint. There shall be provisions for substitutes for people having class responsibilities and reimbursement for professional staff for night meetings. Student(s) involved may attend and should be notified by the IMC in writing.

4.23 The superintendent may request other professionally qualified resource persons to serve with the committee and to be reimbursed.

4.24 The chair of the IMC shall, within 30 calendar days after receipt of the complaint, submit the final recommendation of the IMC to the superintendent.

4.25 The superintendent may accept or reject the IMC's decision. The superintendent shall, within ten (10) calendar days of receiving the IMC decision, notify all concerned of his/her decision.

4.26 The superintendent shall submit a copy of the IMC report to the board and indicate the action he/she is going to take. Materials shall not be removed from use until a final decision, through proper procedural action, has been completed.

4.27 The superintendent's decision shall be reviewed by the board upon a request for appeal from any of the concerned parties. Such request of the board must be made within ten (10) calendar days of receipt of the superintendent's decision. (If a request is not received by the board within the ten calendar days, the challenge process shall be completed.)

4.28 The board shall review relevant documentation and render their decision within 45 calendar days.

4.29 People who feel the board decision warrants further consideration shall appeal through appropriate legal channels.

5. SURVIVAL TIPS FOR CONDUCTING AN INSTRUCTIONAL MEDIA COMMITTEE HEARING ON CHALLENGED MATERIALS

Planning

1. The IMC chairperson, in cooperation with appropriate district personnel, establishes the hearing date, place, time in strict accordance with district policy requirements.
2. All affected persons (complainant, teacher(s), principal, superintendent, the board, media, etc.) are notified, in writing, regarding the hearing.
3. All affected people (above) also receive with their notification, a listing or statement of expectations and limitations regarding the hearings procedure, which may include the following:

   - Verbal presentations will be limited to three minutes (districts may want to extend or shorten this time).
   - Testimony is to be limited to the material under consideration only.
   - No personal attacks will be allowed.
   - Time allocations will be monitored strictly.
   - Testimony is to be directed to the committee and not other members of the audience.
   - The audience may not question or interrupt a person giving testimony.
   - The press/media is requested to arrive early to set up equipment.
   - Written testimony should not exceed four, double spaced, typewritten pages and the content must be directed to the material under consideration and it must not contain personal attacks or allegations. Set a specific due date.
   - Those choosing to give testimony must notify the school district, in writing. (Set a specific date and time that is in accordance with policy and that will allow the committee to get a perspective of the number of participants.)

4. The IMC chairperson will set a time limitation on the overall public testimony portion of the hearing. Ideally, one hour is best, but the time is related to the number of persons indicating they would like to participate.

Physical Setting

1. The IMC should be seated at tables, preferably at an elevated level, facing the audience.
2. Provide theater-style seating for the audience, if possible.

3. Microphones should be available if the room is large.
4. A table or podium is necessary for the people giving testimony.
5. Have a clock (that the chairperson can easily see) or a stop watch. Some community organization or the school debate team may have the ''debate lights'' that are red, yellow and green and provide speakers a visual indicator of their time allocation.
6. Video, audio and or media equipment should be set up in advance to eliminate disruptions.
7. Notepads, pencils and glasses of water should be provided for the committee.

Hearing Procedures

1. Introduce the committee.
2. State the purpose of the hearing in accordance with district policies and procedures.
3. Review the procedures that will be followed, specifically all those issues contained in the notification letters.
4. Order of testimony may vary. Suggestions include:
   • Random drawing of names;
   • Alternating opponents and proponents;
   • Having all opponents testify first, then all of the proponents follow.
5. Consistently and firmly maintain control of speakers' time, audience interruptions, inappropriate testimony, etc.
6. If any person shows total disregard for the rules, and after sufficient warnings, the chairperson has the option of discontinuing / recessing the hearing until the person/people leave or regain control of themselves.

Taking Testimony

1. Request that speakers give their name and address at the onset of their presentation.
2. Again, firmly and fairly monitor time and inappropriate comments, audience interacton, etc.
3. Remind speakers to address the committee, not the audience and to focus their comments on the specific book, film, etc.

Closing Testimony

1. Thank all participants.
2. Briefly explain the next part of the IMC process is that the committee will review and discuss comments, research, professional litera-

ture, etc. The audience may stay and listen, **but they may not participate or interrupt the committee during deliberations.**

Conducting the IMC Deliberations

1. Chairperson will lead committee members in a review of testimony and relevant information focusing on identifying salient points of agreement and disagreement.
2. Issues should be kept within the confines of district policy, state law, the collective bargaining agreement and educational precedence.
3. Prioritize issues.
4. Explore alternatives.
5. Avoid giving credence to anecdotal "evidence."
6. Take a vote and record how each committee member voted.
7. If the committee cannot reach a decision or if they feel they need additional information, the chairperson may choose to set a continuance. (This necessitates notifications, adherence to timeline restrictions, etc.)
8. When the committee reaches a decision, members' votes and specific suggestions are recorded (see the "IMC Recommendation Form" on the next page) and forwarded to the appropriate people and organizations (e.g., complainant, teacher(s), principal, superintendent, board, media).

Instructional Materials Committee
Hearing Recommendations

Date of Hearing: _____

Location of Hearing: _____

Title of Challenged Material: _____

Author: _____

Publisher: _____

Date of Publication: _____

Where in the district is this material currently being used (or is located)?

_____

Request initiated by: _____

The challenged material is classified by the IMC as: (check those that apply)

_____ Textbook

_____ Supplemental classroom material

_____ Library book

_____ Film / video

_____ Specific educational program

_____ Educational resource kit

_____ Magazine

_____ Class handout / activity.

The specific issue to be resolved at this hearing: _____

_____

_____

_____

_____

Findings of Fact: _____

_____

_____

_____

_____

_____

_____

_____

_____

Recommendations (Continued)

Summation of the decision of the committee: _____

_____
_____
_____
_____
_____
_____
_____
_____
_____
_____
_____
_____
_____
_____

IMC Membership Names: Vote Record:

_____(Chair)   ____ Yes ____ No
_____   ____ Yes ____ No
_____   ____ Yes ____ No
_____   ____ Yes ____ No
_____   ____ Yes ____ No
_____   ____ Yes ____ No
_____   ____ Yes ____ No
_____   ____ Yes ____ No

Submitted this date _____
by _____
                        (IMC Chairperson)

Copies to:

_____
_____
_____
_____
_____
_____
_____
_____

Request for Reconsideration

Please complete this form and submit it to (designated administrator: _____
by (date): _____

Author: _____ Title: _____

Text: ____ Library book: ____ Magazine: ____ Film / video: ____ Other: ____

Publisher: _____ Publication Date: _____

Request initiated by: _____
Street Address: _____
City: _____ State: _____ZIP: _____ Phone:_____

Citizen represents:
_____ Self
_____ Organization (identify) _____
_____ Other group (identify) _____

1. To what in the book or material do you object? Please cite specific pages.
_____

2. Why do you object to the use of this material?
_____
_____
_____

3. Have you read or viewed the entire contents? ____ Yes ____ No

4. What pages or portions did you read or view? _____

5. What would you like your school to do about this material?
      _____ Do not assign or recommend it to my child.
      _____ Place on restricted use (parental approval required).
      _____ Other: _____
    Comments: _____
             _____
             _____

District Policy (number) _____ and related Procedures (number) _____ detail the processes and timelines that will be followed upon receipt of this form by the above named administrator. Copies of these policies and procedures are available upon request.

_____   _____ 19 _____
           Signature   Date

For District Use: Date Received: _____ By Whom? _____